Beating the F.E.A.R. Factor

15 Minutes to Your Ideal Retirement

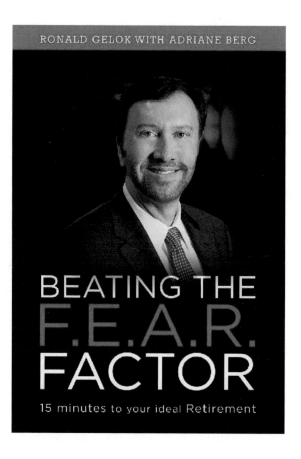

RONALD GELOK WITH ADRIANE BERG

BEATING THE
F.E.A.R.
FACTOR
15 minutes to your ideal Retirement

**By Ronald Gelok
with Adriane Berg**

ISBN Number: 978-1-4951-4541-4

The views, opinions, and ideas expressed in this book are solely those of the author, Ronald Gelok. They are not necessarily those of any organization, corporation, entity, or person with whom the author presently has, in the past has had, or may in the future have a business connection.

Library of Congress Cataloging-in-Publication Data

Gelok, Ronald.

ISBN NO: 978-1-4951-4541-4 Beating the F.E.A.R. Factor, 15 Minutes to Your Ideal Retirement – First edition.

This book is available at special quantity discounts for use as premiums and sales promotions or for use in corporate training programs. To contact a representative, please e-mail adrianeberg@msn.com.

By RONALD GELOK, with Adriane Berg

Acknowledgments

Thank You From Ron:

I want to thank my family for believing in me and allowing me the many hours of time necessary to complete this manuscript.

I also want to thank the dedicated staff and advisors at Ronald Gelok & Associates for providing above-and-beyond exemplary client service.

I want to thank my fans and friends, the clients of Ronald Gelok & Associates, all of whom I collectively pictured as I wrote this book and who were the abiding inspiration for everything you will read.

I want to thank Steve Forbes for the opportunity to be a contributing author to the best-selling book *Successonomics*.

I want to thank estate planning attorney Tom Smith, my co-author for my first best-selling book, *Retirement Rescue*.

Finally, I want to thank Adriane Berg, a worthy sounding board for my ideas and prolific contributor to this book.

Thank You From Adriane:

First, I would like to thank Ronald Gelok for opening the door to a better future for all of us through his comforting and sound financial information.

I would like to thank my husband and business partner, Stuart Bochner, and apologize to him for his 43 years of suffering through my crazy ideas and massive undertakings; and for editing and designing the pages of this book to add visual clarity to what Ron and I write.

I want to thank the hard-working staff at Ronald Gelok & Associates, especially Morgan Kelly Curran, Patricia Nealy, and Leslie Toner, without whom this book would be a thought and not a reality.

Finally, I want to thank my listeners, viewers, and readers who have followed my work since 1980 and unaccountably have asked for more.

By RONALD GELOK, with Adriane Berg

Table of Contents

Forward by Adriane Berg

Introduction: How to Use This Book

Chapter 1

15 Minutes to Your Ideal Retirement: No, It's Not Impossible

What you will discover: What *F.E.A.R. Factor* really stands for and how we are duped into a fearful and worry-filled financial position at retirement through mistaken beliefs on tax deferral, investing, and other "sensible" herd mentality strategies

We cover:

> ➢ Determining your ideal retirement
>
> ➢ Finding your retirement soft spots
>
> ➢ Shaking the "herd" mentality

What to do next:

> ➢ DREAM: Imagine your ideal retirement.
>
> ➢ Visit www.fearfactorthebook.com and get our hints and tips on answering the *7 Big Questions*.

Chapter 2

How to Lead the Tax-Free Retirement Lifestyle

We cover: How a tax-free retirement lifestyle can be the same as putting 33% extra buying power in your pocket.

What you will discover:

> ➢ How taxable income, including distributions from pension and other plans, are diminished by taxes

---

By RONALD GELOK, with Adriane Berg

➤ Tax-free lifestyle also means low state income tax, sales tax, estate tax, luxury tax, property tax

➤ A map of different types of taxes in different states in the United States

➤ Why prepaying tax may be the hidden secret of an ideal retirement

What to do next:

➤ Take a "guesstimate" as to your tax bracket after retirement. If you like DIY, there are calculators to use at www.fearfactorthebook.com. If you want our help, visit that site and get your complimentary review.

Chapter 3

What's the difference between a plan and a system?

We cover: A plan is what most people think about when it comes to retirement—that's why so few people actually plan for retirement. Not only is it tedious, scary, and unfocused, but it often makes you face questions that you have a very hard time answering. A system answers the question of how much you will have to live on. Then it's easier to make choices about how you want to live.

You will discover:

➤ How to answer planners when they ask "Where would you like to live? What lifestyle do you envision after retirement?" Not only are these questions difficult to answer, but couples may have different answers, and everyone changes their answers a year or two or more after retirement. Yet, almost every retirement plan asks you how much you need to live in retirement. How should you know?

➤ The best answer: "I'll live on the maximum amount of money I possibly can without running out before I leave this earth."

➤ Why people don't plan for retirement: no plan can help you see into the future. That's why you are likely to spend more time planning your vacation than planning your retirement. It's not because you're bad, it's because you're not clairvoyant.

By RONALD GELOK, with Adriane Berg

> With a system, we look at what you have today and maximize it as much as we possibly can. One essential strategy is to eliminate taxation.

What to do next:

> The first part of creating our system is to determine the "income gap," the gap between what's needed to live your ideal retirement lifestyle and what you have in fixed guaranteed income. Visit www.fearfactorthebook.com to determine your income gap.

> Review the elements of your ideal retirement again at www.fearfactorthebook.com

Chapter 4

Why Is Tax-Free So Much Better Than Tax-Deferred?

We cover: Most Americans have been indoctrinated into the belief that paying taxes later rather than sooner is better for them. Initially this makes sense. If you are growing your wealth and don't have to pay taxes, then all of the gains are growing without diminishment by taxation. Over long periods of time, this does work out well. A time comes, however—anywhere from 10 to 5 years before retirement—when, for many, it no longer pays to defer taxes. It is better to pay the tax and invest tax-free from then on.

You will discover:

> How to determine when to convert your tax-deferred holdings into after-tax holdings

> How to withdraw funds from qualified accounts and pay the tax

> What the ins and outs of the Roth IRA are

> The ins and outs of the system through indexed products

What to do next:

> Go to www.fearfactorthebook.com and you will find our calculator for a guesstimate of your future taxation. By the way,

you will also get a good idea of the income you will have at retirement to determine a ballpark figure of your income gap, if any.

> ➤ If you have an insurance policy with cash value, check out our exchange article on www.fearfactorthebook.com.

Chapter 5

The Pact With the Devil: Stock Market Volatility and Retirement

We cover: A perfect storm is brewing. I am concerned not only with stock market volatility or the next bear market, but also with bond market volatility. Interest rates are at a 30-year low by some standards; as interest rates creep up, fixed income or bonds are going to go backwards. There are solutions to escape excessive volatility by putting the correct system in place.

You will discover:

> ➤ The difference between a managed account and a separately managed account and why you need the latter

> ➤ The reasons for asset allocation and diversification and why those strategies alone don't work to create the ideal retirement

> ➤ Solutions that protect you from devastating market volatility

What to do next:

> ➤ How about getting an illustration especially for you? Register for a private consultation and illustration at www.fearfactorthebook.com

Chapter 6

Would You Like to Build a Tax-Free Money Machine?

We cover: There is more than one way to create the tax-free money machine. Each takes under 15 minutes. You will have to choose between three types of systems to see which sits best with your philosophy. You may want some of each system.

You will discover:

> ➢ Tax-free money machine systems

> ➢ The three systems

> ➢ How to choose

> ➢ Spend 15 minutes to create your future

> ➢ Annuity and insurance riders

What to do next:

> ➢ Visit www.fearfactorthebook.com and check off the riders in which you are interested in learning more.

Chapter 7

Why do *YOU* F.E.A.R. to think outside the box and follow the herd instead?

We cover: The stories of the four people you meet in retirement, using them as iconic models of how the system works in real life. You will learn why you need to think outside the box and not follow the herd.

You will discover:

> ➢ Why you go along with the herd

> ➢ Take a look around. The herd is not doing very well.

> ➢ Most people think inside the box. They saved in 401(k)s if they were disciplined. And even then they paid taxes. They also suffered recession after recession.

> ➢ By following the herd over and over again, we act through fear and act too late.

> ➢ Each and every time we follow the herd, we damage our financial success.

> ➤ Our systems using indexed products do not follow the herd. You might call them contrarian, and if you act in a contrarian manner you should be proud of conquering the F.E.A.R.

What to do next:

> ➤ Please visit www.fearfactorthebook.com for real-life examples of people who perhaps could be your new reference point, your new herd. These are the stories of people who did not get scared by a word but got engaged in really thinking about why they are doing what they're doing.

Chapter 8

How Many Thousands Per Month Tax-Free Do You Want?

We cover: Worksheets to determine how much to convert from tax-free to tax-deferred, based on how much income you want after retirement.

You will discover:

A review of the points made in Chapters 1–7

What to do next:

> ➤ Fill out the worksheets found at www.fearfactorthebook.com and see what's right for you.

Chapter 9

Can We Really Stack the Deck in Our Favor?

We cover: Here's how you stack the deck.
> ➤ You get tax-free income.
> ➤ You get a floor under which your assets can never fall.
> ➤ You retain the power to take an advance on the death benefit insurance portion of your system should you need long-term care.
> ➤ You leave a legacy.
> ➤ You have a guarantee against market volatility.
> ➤ You get market gains participation.
> ➤ You can get market index-linked interest.

The deck is stacked in your favor, but it takes nerve. It takes nerve to pay taxes early, which has always been contrary to the conventional wisdom. It takes nerve to invest in the stock market through a system rather than through individual mutual funds and ETFs. It takes nerve to look at your financial future, face the potential shortfall, and actually do something about it.

You will discover:

> ➢ Proof that controlling loss and minimizing taxes is the name of the game

> ➢ Numbers showing how one couple with herd mentality did against another couple who prepaid taxes and had a guarantee against loss

> ➢ Scenarios for single individuals

> ➢ Early use of insurance benefits for long-term care

What to do next:

> ➢ Visit our website, www.fearfactorthebook.com; you will find very streamlined, simple paperwork. If you'd really like to create your retirement future in 15 minutes, fill out those sheets and get them to us. You'll see instructions on how to do that. Have an in-office or virtual conference with Ronald Gelok & Associates, where trust is built and questions are answered.

Chapter 10

Is There Really a Way to Keep What's Earned in Good Years and Not Lose in Bad Years?

We cover: What is the guarantee for earnings, what is the guarantee of no loss, what is the guarantee of tax-free borrowing, and what is the guarantee of early use of insurance proceeds?

You will discover:

> ➢ The criticism of the system—what is fair and what is not
> ➢ Criticisms include high commissions and fees, phony guarantees, and what to look for to protect yourself
> ➢ How the Gelok team protects you

By RONALD GELOK, with Adriane Berg

What to do next:

> ➢ Review the easy worksheets www.fearfactorthebook.com.

Chapter 11

What Kind of Team Do You Need to Navigate the Shark-Infested Waters That Lie Ahead?

We cover: An introduction to creating the ideal financial team, how the Gelok team can help, and which ancillary professionals you might need to add to your team.

You will discover:

> ➢ What fee treachery awaits you?
>
> ➢ How long-term care problems can be solved—and NOT just financial issues
>
> ➢ How to avoid retirement pitfalls
>
> ➢ Beyond, money—how a great retirement means life purpose, good health and spiritual wealth
>
> ➢ Good stewardship for legacy building

What to do next:

> ➢ Meet our team: Check out www.fearfactorthebook.com. Create your Family Financial Tree and meet our family.

Chapter 12

How Does Overcoming F.E.A.R. and Making Smart Decisions in Your Money Life Spill Over to All of Your Retirement Decisions?

We cover: You will be amazed at how rapidly formerly unsolvable issues, like where and when you want to retire and what you will do after retirement, will be solved once you have a perpetual financial system that never runs out of money no matter how long you live.

You will discover:

➤ A review of F.E.A.R. as it relates to money

➤ How F.E.A.R. also relates to other issues

➤ How dancing to your own drummer and believing in yourself is essential to a free and amazing retirement

➤ How vanquishing the F.E.A.R. Factors inspires others

What to do next:

➤ Read some of the outstanding books and visit the websites in Appendix xx and get inspired.

Chapter 13

How Does Discovering Your Financial Blind Spots Lead to Making Better Financial Decisions?

What we cover: We are all unable to see certain dangers in our plan. When they are noted, we can take care of them and we can prosper. What we don't see are our blind spots, and they can destroy our retirement. Let's identify the most frequent blind spots.

What you will discover: The big blind spots:
➤ taxes
➤ risk
➤ income gap
➤ catastrophic illness

What to do next:

➤ Visit www.RonaldGelok.com./F.E.A.R.Factor. You'll discover your blind spots. I assure you it's going to be a real eye-opener.

Chapter 14

Epilogue: Take the F.E.A.R. Factor Quiz
            Register for the F.E.A.R. Factor Webinar Series

Introduction: How to Use this Book

This book presents a single, simple concept. You can craft a stress-free financial future if you are open to owning certain very specialized products designed to

- Guarantee that your gains will not be lost in bad stock market years
- Participate when the stock market indexes have good years
- Guarantee a specific return on your money that you can count on for income
- Distribute that income tax-free, or tax-advantaged
- Provide a legacy to a loved one
- Give you cash if you need to pay for long-term care expenses so they won't break the bank.
- In other words, create a system that solves the money problems that we normally face after we retire.

Although we spend sufficient time explaining how the system works, this book also primes you to think out of the box, so you can take action.

What you will discover is not the financial planning norm; it requires some personal guidance and education.

Really this is not a book at all. The Internet has given us so much opportunity to interact that what you have before you is a conduit to help and support through our website exercises, forms, webinars, and personal video calling consultations.

At the beginning of each chapter, you will find three sections that will take about a minute to read:

- What we cover
- What you will discover
- What to do next

If you wish, you can skip reading the chapter altogether and go directly to "What to do next," our call to action. We have done this to keep our 15-minute promise.

I know you have no time to plan for the many decades of your life after retirement, but you must. Our system guides you so simply that taking action is inevitable, time-efficient, and painless.

By RONALD GELOK, with Adriane Berg

Yes, there is gain without pain, but only if you are willing to keep an open mind.

You might find this book peculiarly written. That's because I am talking to you personally. I do virtual seminars twice a week, and I am used to speaking with people directly. You will find snippets of real conversations sprinkled throughout the book.

You will also find the details and invitations to my complementary seminars (usually I buy lunch) by calling our office at (800)467-8152. If you are in the New Jersey/New York area, please take advantage of them.

If you are not in the area, become an Ambassador by bringing us to your town to speak to your group. You can do that right now by calling our office at (800)467-8152.

I suggest that you sign up for a seminar or to be an Ambassador right now, even before you read further.

Why the urgency?

Because as we will discuss, the way you do anything is the way you do everything. If you don't train yourself to take advantage of free, no-pressure information, you are in danger of not taking action to create your future.

Say yes to the ideal retirement in baby steps, starting with a complementary seminar or enrolling in the Ambassador program to bring us to you.

By doing so right now, you will have a better chance of doing the exercises you find at the end of some of the chapters. If you do them, you will have created a system for your ideal retirement in 15 minutes.

Enough said. We have 14½ minutes left, so let's get going!

A Note From Adriane

6 Top Reasons Why Beating the F.E.A.R. Factor Is Necessary for Your Bright Future

I swore I would never write another money book. I've written more than a dozen. Honestly, it was time to relax. But when Ronald Gelok asked me to co-write with him, I couldn't refuse. Let me explain. In addition to the respect I have for Ron, I realized there was a lot more to say about personal finance than in my fourteen other books. Yes, they were old, the last written in 2008. And I was young, 66 to be exact.

I realized that if I need NEW information for my successful aging, you might too.

In reflecting on what's new to say, I began to think of what has changed since I started and how the changes affect your retirement. Here are the factors that I find significant today. You be the judge of whether they are part of your F.E.A.R. Factor.

1. Financial Media

I wrote my first book in 1980, *Money Think: Financial Planning Finally Made Easy,* published by a small New York press, Pilgrim Press. In those days, publishers sent you all around the country on book tours to promote your book.

I made many TV and radio guest appearances through the years—*OPRAH* four times, *Good Morning America*, Home Show, Regis, you name it. My son Arthur appeared on Jay Leno twice with our *Totally Awesome Money Book for Kids and Their Family* published by Newmarket Press. I then became host of one of the first cable TV shows, *IRS Tax Beat*, and *Money Talks*, a syndicated radio show.

Lots of people think I'm a pioneer because I came before Suzy Orman, *Mad Money*, or Maria Bartolomo. I spent years breaking the barrier between us and the financial professionals. I insist that personal finance can be understood by the layman investor, who is the backbone of all financial markets.

That's why I feel partly responsible for the good and the bad we have in financial media today. There is more financial news available than ever before. I like that. The news content trades on the usual stock of journalism—bad news. I don't like that. Why? Because bad news can be just as distorted and one-sided as good news. And it sticks faster and more permanently.

When you hear overly good news, put your antenna up and question. Similarly, when you hear overly bad news, do the same. If some TV personality bashes annuities, it may be for very good reasons, to protect you from making a mistake. But it may also be to broadcast a story that riles people up and makes good copy. No one ever gets in trouble telling you NOT to do something.

Just take all the financial news and programs with a grain of salt.

2. The Internet

In 1980 when I wrote my first book, the Internet hardly existed for the average person. Today, I never visit a hotel without looking at Trip Advisor. How about you?

I see pictures of the facility taken by consumers and pictures taken by the promotional people for the hotel, and ubiquitous comments. What influences me is a combination of what the consumer says and what the owners say.

So, too, what laymen say about money and investing is all over the Internet, together with bloggers, economists, and financial gurus. We can't help being educated, influenced, and confused by this plethora of information and opinions.

Money savvy takes experience and expertise. Do-it-yourself websites, many of which I write for every day, are very useful and eye-opening. They are not, however, a substitute for having a true financial professional by your side.

3. The Death of the Pension

I spent a lot of pages in past books explaining strategies regarding how and when to take a pension. You won't find that in this book. I haven't written about this strategy in almost a decade. Why? **Because there are no pensions left!**

That means we are on our own to save in qualified plans, invest right, and withdraw right. Very scary. Yet the art and science of making the most of your money at the endgame stage is often overlooked.

By RONALD GELOK, with Adriane Berg

What must we know when it's time to withdraw retirement funds? This is what this book is about.

It suggests some NEW ways of thinking. Ways I have never written about before, because most of America was in the accumulation stage. Now with 10,000 people reaching age 65 each day, there are 78 million Baby Boomers ready to pay attention.

4. My House Is Underwater

In the old days, anyone who said their house was underwater was talking about a flood. Today, it means that our home is worth less than the mortgage on the property, or the equity is a fraction of what we thought it would be. We are questioning the wisdom of a fundamental of the American Dream—owning your own home.

Take Willy Loman, the protagonist in my favorite American play, *Death of a Salesman.* In the end Willy kills himself because he was marginalized and felt useless (and for a few other reasons), all brought down to his failure as a man. At his funeral, his wife turns to a friend and says (to paraphrase), "Why did he do that? We just paid off the mortgage."

Yes, owning a home was the quintessential life goal of every American, made more important by our immigrants, many of whom were not allowed home ownership in the country from which they fled.

No more. Now the discussion is how to hold on long enough to get your equity out. Willy would probably have been better off living and doing a short sale.

5. Longevity

In 2010 I started Generation Bold to help businesses market to boomers, older adults, and caregivers. I never use the word *senior*, because I don't know what that means.

We are a fungible generation; our lifestyle is more determined by our mental health, physical health, financial health, creativity, and flexibility than our chronological age.

My radio show is no longer about money; it's called *Generation Bold* and can be heard on BizTalkRadio.

By RONALD GELOK, with Adriane Berg

We talk about sex, money, health, travel, working, writing novels after 60, starting a business after 70, indulging grandkids, late-life divorce, late-life marriage, fashion—and did I mention sex?

We are as old as we want to be. Cynics might add that we are as young as we can afford to be.

At many of my speaking engagements, I tell a joke:

"There's good news and bad news. The good news is you're going to live longer. The bad news is you can't afford it."

Outliving your money is no joke. I've seen it with my own eyes. People who could be thriving at home but made no provision for a long-term illness now sit in wheelchairs at nursing homes because they ran out of money. Every Mother's Day I bring gifts to nursing homes. Every year I am appalled at how few visitors the residents have, even on this special day. By contrast, I see people with disabilities using walkers, portable oxygen, traveling with companions to Europe, and taking cruises. I started www.TheAgelessTraveler.com so people could travel at any age. Thousands do.

Here's the terrible fact: The people traveling and having a full life despite infirmity have the same diagnoses as the people in wheelchairs. What happened? They took a different path because of the money available to support their lifestyle. Bette Davis said, "Old age is not for sissies." Anyone who denies the possibility of chronic illness is a sissy. Please prepare for it.

Now, cheer up. Most people do not get Alzheimer's, Parkinson's disease, or a stroke. They live long and prosper. That too works best if you are willing to embrace your aging and make the most of a GOOD THING. It's your time to shine, do what you want, be unafraid; paint, write, teach, volunteer. Be prepared for the greatest life phase ever.

6. Stock Market Correlation

Today, most retirement planning boils down to a pie chart of allocated assets with internal diversification. The theory, which you will read more about later in this book, was proven historically. It simply states:

Different asset classes react differently to market influencers, so if you diversify within and among asset classes, you are more protected.

By RONALD GELOK, with Adriane Berg

Except things have changed and assets have become much more correlated. Stocks, bonds, precious metals, commodities and even real estate all go up and down in more lockstep than ever before. You are less protected than you think when you merely asset allocate.

Why is the asset allocation strategy eroding? I believe that the media influence, hard news, and consumer temperament is so powerful now that all financial decisions are reacting to the same factors. I also believe that money managers, especially of funds, are now so scrutinized (a good thing) that they stop thinking for themselves (a bad thing). Star-quality fund managers were rock stars in the 1980s and 1990s. Today it's all about programmed trading and what the computer tells you to do. Naturally, the computer tells everyone the same thing. So let's play safe, say the managers. No manager gets faulted if they make the same mistake as every other manager.

For you, this simply means you need to work harder to protect your net worth. Asset allocation alone, although still very important, is not enough.

By RONALD GELOK, with Adriane Berg

Chapter 1

15 Minutes to Your Ideal Retirement: No, It's Not Impossible

I know that taking only 15 minutes to achieve your ideal retirement sounds impossible, but it's not. It's not if you're thinking the right way and if you're not frozen by fear. Fear of the ability to retire has been in the news constantly for baby boomers, the mature, and particularly for Millennials. You may have heard that you will need millions to retire, that healthcare will break the bank, and you're in for a lifetime of asking, "Do you want fries with that?"

Nonsense. Bad news sells. All you will get from the media is bad news.

Here's the good news: You're going to live longer, and you can afford it.

You're about to get an earful about real-world retirement, and that earful is going to change your life. So, in the next 15 minutes, set aside your fears. After all, this is just a book with an interactive website. You're not in any danger. Sure, my task is to help you change your thinking, and that can cause anxiety. But in this case it will also deliver an anxiety-free future.

Funny, but many people don't want to hear that things are good, that money will be enough. They get suspicious of anyone offering good news but accept unquestioningly the bad news.

Now, that type of defeatist thinking is dangerous in three important ways we will address right now.

1. When you fear to dream, your dreams disappear or morph into a watered-down version of what you really want.

Many of us beat down our retirement before we get started. We procrastinate on taking action, or even making a plan. We are loath to compromise, and we start with the assumption that we must compromise.

When you first saw the title of this book, you were probably interested in the 15-minute aspect. That's about all we are willing to spend to manage the 30-plus years after retirement that the average American gets. Why so little thought to so long a life stage?

By RONALD GELOK, with Adriane Berg

Because the important word in our title is the word *ideal*. What's an ideal retirement? For most of us it's the retirement we are pretty sure we can't have! Who wants to plan for a less than ideal retirement? Not you, or me either.

Let's at least pretend that an ideal retirement is possible. Play along with me. Resist the temptation to curtail your dreams and be "realistic." Open your heart to what you'd love to do in retirement, where you dream to live, and the personal and financial legacy you want to leave.

Be crazy, just for 2 minutes, and write down what an ideal retirement would look like to you. Write down the basics: where you would live and how would you spend your day, and with whom you would spend it.

Picture your ideal day in retirement. What would you like to do in the morning each day after you have your coffee? That's all you need to know to have the ideal retirement. After that we can do the rest together and make it happen.

Did you write it down yet? No. I'll wait. So are you finding it hard to get started? Or are you confused as to what an ideal retirement is to you? Or do you have too many answers? Or are you worried because your significant other wants something different?

By RONALD GELOK, with Adriane Berg

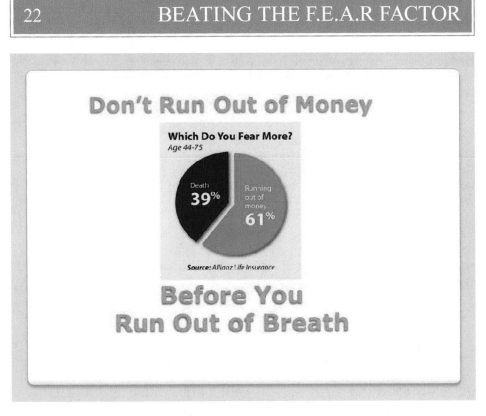

Congratulations, you just met the F.E.A.R. Factor.

Okay. What's the F.E.A.R. Factor? It's an acronym. Here's what it means and how it affects your retirement planning:

Most people think of F.E.A.R., the acronym, as False Evidence Appearing Real. I look at it a little bit differently. I think it stands for **False Evidence Affecting Retirement**, and I think we've been brainwashed a little bit by the media into thinking in certain fearful ways that are ultimately destructive to our retirement.

Now, some of these fears we all recognize instinctively as practically universal—for example, the fear of running out of money before we run out of breath.

First-time clients come into my office and they're fearful about the future. They just don't know what they should be doing with their retirement savings. They know they don't want to keep it in "certificates of disappointment," CDs, that are yielding next to no interest.

By RONALD GELOK, with Adriane Berg

They're scared to death of having too much in bonds or fixed income because, as interest rates go up, we know that bonds are likely to plummet in value. And there's also the concern, with the stock market being so high, of going through another "correction" like the ones in 2001, 2002, and 2008.

Of course, the fear of market pullback in a bull market is very real. The statistics on how often the stock market goes into recession are scary. It's hard to crawl your way back up, particularly if you're on a fixed income. Typically twice per decade or every six to seven years we may hit a recession or a bear market where we can lose a significant portion of our retirement savings.

Today, most people would agree that they can't afford to go through another 2008 or another bear market. If you think back to 2008, the equity markets plunged 39%, almost 40%. You needed a 67% increase just to get your money back to where it started, which took years. If you're knocking on the door of retirement, you don't have years. You won't get a do-over if you don't get it right this time.

The Mathematics of Stock Market Recovery

Decline Amount	Advance Required to Breakeven
25%	33%
33%	50%
50%	100%
75%	300%
90%	900%

By RONALD GELOK, with Adriane Berg

2. If you are caught between fear of the market and disgust over low interest rates, you are probably stuck at making financial decisions and are in danger of "following the herd."

Studies show most of the portfolios of retired people look exactly the same. So this herd mentality is hurting us, but from where does it come and what can we do about it?

I think it comes from a number of different factors. Certainly we are creatures of habit. We do things the way we always do them simply because that's the way we've always done them. I'm guilty of this too in my personal life.

It feels safe. For example, people will position a 401(k) or a retirement account at age 60 the same way they did when they were 40 years old. They'll be too heavily weighted towards risk-based securities where they're likely to suffer major losses in the next market downturn.

You must make the distinction between accumulation mode, preservation mode, and distribution mode.

> ➢ Accumulation Mode—20 years or more before retirement during which it's okay to take some risks to build wealth

> ➢ Preservation Mode—5 or so years before retirement during which you must be sure you don't go backward but can still take chances on a lesser portion of assets

> ➢ Distribution Mode—At and after retirement when you can't lose anything and must count on a monthly or quarterly sum without a paycheck

If you truly want the ideal retirement, you must start making adjustments to how you hold and regard your assets. That includes your qualified plans and savings.

Just as a time comes when you decide to retire or to downsize your home, you should also change the way you think about your portfolio, because you're going into a new life stage.

A major example is how you manage your taxes. Being tax-savvy is as important, maybe more, after you retire than when you are working.

By RONALD GELOK, with Adriane Berg

My training was as a tax and estate planning attorney, but don't hold that against me.

I started my career doing wills and trusts, helping people plan to minimize the amount of estate taxes that would go to the government at their passing. I saw back in the late 1990s and early 2000s that, as people's assets evaporated during the dot-com bubble burst and after 9/11, the correct estate planning and all the right legal documents did no good when money was disappearing or losing value.

No More Money in the Mailbox

In my trusts and estates law practice, I naturally worked with many post-retirees. If you think about it, most people that do estate planning are older people. Now should younger people do it? Of course; everyone who has children, for example, should have a will.

However, not surprisingly my clients were mostly retired already. One thing I observed more than 20 years ago was that most of my clients had true pensions, paychecks for life, guaranteed income, and mailbox money every month.

As they say in my great state of New Jersey, 'Fuggedaboudit!'

Most baby boomers and those younger have IRAs or 401ks, 457s, or 403bs, but not pensions. The "Silent Generation," our current post-retirees, many of whom never made the income we make today, are actually better able to retire than younger generations.

One statistic I saw recently cites that only 16% of people retiring today are retiring with traditional defined benefit pensions. This creates a huge problem that we need to solve—the "income gap," or the gap between what's guaranteed in the way of Social Security and other income and what we need to cover our post-retirement expenses. And it's not just expenses today; it's expenses tomorrow. So inflation is a factor.

By RONALD GELOK, with Adriane Berg

A Note From Adriane

Of Course, Inflation Is Not a Big Factor as We Age
One thing I can tell you as a marketer reaching boomers, the mature adult, and caregivers, a lot of companies don't want to bother reaching us at all. Why? They don't think we spend any money. They have the "depression mentality by proxy." They keep thinking we are the older type of senior citizen, not the new type of go-go years active adult. The fact is we do spend, and some of what we buy, like health care, has higher inflation than what the average Consumer Price Index shows. There is an Elder Consumer Price Index, and it warns us that inflation is in our future.

Here is an excerpt from *Congressional Budget Office, How Does Growth in the Cost of Goods and Services for the Elderly Compare to That for the Overall Population?* by Noah Meyerson an analyst in CBO's Health, Retirement, and Long-Term Analysis Division, and David Brauer, an analyst in CBO's Macroeconomic Analysis Division.

Read it and weep:

"The possibility that the cost of living may grow at a different rate for the elderly than for the rest of the population is of particular concern in choosing a price index for Social Security cost-of-living adjustments because Social Security benefits are the main source of income for many older people. Bureau of Labor Statistics (BLS) computes an unofficial index that reflects the purchasing patterns of older people, called the experimental CPI for Americans 62 years of age and older (CPI-E). Since 1982 (the earliest date for which that index has been computed), annual inflation as measured by the CPI-E has been 0.2 percentage points higher, on average, than inflation as measured by the traditional CPI-U or the CPI-W.

By RONALD GELOK, with Adriane Berg

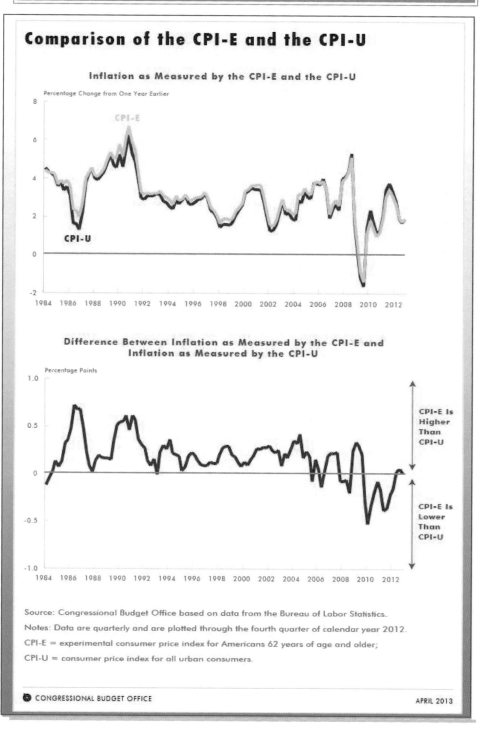

Comparison of the CPI-E and the CPI-U

Inflation as Measured by the CPI-E and the CPI-U

Percentage Change from One Year Earlier

CPI-E

CPI-U

1984 1986 1988 1990 1992 1994 1996 1998 2000 2002 2004 2006 2008 2010 2012

Difference Between Inflation as Measured by the CPI-E and Inflation as Measured by the CPI-U

Percentage Points

CPI-E Is Higher Than CPI-U

CPI-E Is Lower Than CPI-U

1984 1986 1988 1990 1992 1994 1996 1998 2000 2002 2004 2006 2008 2010 2012

Source: Congressional Budget Office based on data from the Bureau of Labor Statistics.

Notes: Data are quarterly and are plotted through the fourth quarter of calendar year 2012.

CPI-E = experimental consumer price index for Americans 62 years of age and older;

CPI-U = consumer price index for all urban consumers.

CONGRESSIONAL BUDGET OFFICE

APRIL 2013

By RONALD GELOK, with Adriane Berg

The longer-term difference between the growth rates of the CPI-E and CPI-U mainly reflects the fact that a larger percentage of spending by the elderly is for items whose prices rise especially quickly. In particular, compared with the overall population, the elderly devote a much larger percentage of their spending to medical care. That difference in spending patterns alone accounts for about half of the long-run difference between the CPI-E and the CPI U.

The other half of the longer-term difference between the growth rates of the CPI-E and CPI-U occurs primarily because other goods and services that receive greater emphasis in the CPI-E have prices that tend to rise at an above-average rate—most notably, housing. Over the past five years, however, the CPI for housing has risen less than the overall CPI has. That situation may be at least partly attributable to the collapse in housing prices that largely resulted from overbuilding during the previous economic boom. Because housing prices have started to rise again and we expect that increase to continue in the coming decade, we anticipate that the CPI-E will outpace the CPI-U in the future."

You can't invest like you are living in the past and yet secure your future. If you do that, you might outlive your money.

That's a real risk today. The fastest-growing segment of our population is age 85+, and one startling statistic is that 2 out of 3 of the 85+ population are women. We see it all the time where a husband passes away, and if he had a pension, the pension might be cut by a half or by a third for the surviving spouse.

Then there's the loss of one of the Social Security checks. It's so important today to do planning beyond just following an asset allocation model.

The "follow the herd" mentality gives you pie charts for asset allocations, and there we stand like Alice in Wonderland puzzled at which road to take. So we follow the herd, as we've always done it that way.

How can we, as individuals, knowing that we have to plan for a much longer future think differently so that we do change our habits and we do it fast? After all, this is F.E.A.R. Factor: 15 Minutes to an Ideal Retirement, not 15 years to an ideal retirement.

Here's how:

By RONALD GELOK, with Adriane Berg

Answer these questions if you want to meet the 15-minute deadline

➤ Question one: How much can I afford to lose?

➤ Question two: How much income am I going to need in the first two years after retirement or semiretirement?

➤ Question three: What happens if I have a change in health status down the road? How would I cover those expenses?

➤ Question four: What if my plan A doesn't work out as expected? What's the plan B?

➤ Question five: How can I make sure my surviving spouse is going to be okay?

➤ Question six: If I'm interested in leaving a legacy, how do I provide for that?

➤ Question number seven: How do I keep the government or the taxman's hands OUT of my pockets as much as I legally can?

I call these the *7 Big Questions*. Answer those questions for yourself and for me. Don't be afraid to tackle the answers. What I want you to determine is where you are stuck. Once you know, the answers will come and you will focus on the right things.

For example, if you are happy with your death benefit insurance and feel your spouse will be okay, you cut that out of your concerns. Review your insurance once a year, but otherwise you're good there. If you determine that too much of your assets are in risk-related investments, you need to concentrate on making your portfolio more secure.

You need not come up with the solutions now, just the issues. If you're having trouble, visit www.fearfactorthebook.com and get our hints and tips on answering the *7 Big Questions*.

By RONALD GELOK, with Adriane Berg

A Note From Adriane

The Saber-Toothed Tiger and F.E.A.R. Factor

I have a theory about why money is so emotional—why, in making what should be hard-headed decisions, we "run with the herd." Whether I'm right or wrong, working out this theory has cleared my head to make the right money moves. The theory gets to the center of this book, so stick with me.

Scientists agree the amygdala is the most primitive part of the brain. It engenders the fight/flight response. If you sense danger, you will either fight or flee. Either way, your adrenal fluid spills out into your system and your heart races. You are under stress.

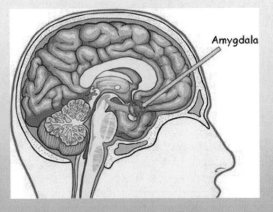

In caveman days the stress was almost always physical, like the danger of a saber-toothed tiger or woolly mammoth devouring you or trampling you to death.

Many choose to flee, to actually run away with the herd of other men. Greater hunters fought and either died or had a good meal to bring home to cave #76.

Where are today's saber-toothed tigers and woolly mammoths? Actually they are everywhere. In traffic jams, at the office, in what you imagine might happen in the back seat of your daughter's boyfriend's car, and certainly in your bank account, stock account, and net worth. There are some that say not listening to the news will add three years to your life, as bad news causes an amygdala hijack and stress and adrenaline overload. In small quantities, over time, that shortens lifespan.

By RONALD GELOK, with Adriane Berg

Scientists are pretty much in agreement with all this, but here is my extra spin.

I believe that negative thoughts are far more powerful in influencing behavior than positive thoughts. Thoughts are largely there to PROTECT you. Protection usually means STOPPING BEHAVIOR, not encouraging behavior. Safety is hard to come by, whether you are a businessman or woman, or a caveman or woman.

F.E.A.R., as we mean it in this book, alludes to false evidence affecting your retirement decisions and ultimately the way you will live in retirement. That false evidence is usually negative, meant to protect you and stop you from acting.

F.E.A.R. in this sense is very powerful. False negative evidence is often very well intentioned, making it even more powerful as an influencer. The government has spent time and money making sure you are protected from overly positive messages. For example, no financial professional or company can say that "past performance is evidence of future performance." This protects you from the illusion that if an investment went well in the past it will be good in the future. This is good protection, but it protects from a positive thought.

Of course, we should prohibit exaggeration, hyperbole, failure to tell all the details, and all the ways nefarious people sell bad investments. By all means, protect yourself against exuberance.

But what about the opposite? I live in a world where I am constantly with multimillionaires, even billionaires. Every investment they make turns to gold. How did they get started on such a path to riches? For the most part they believed in themselves, did not follow anyone else, and were simply less scared to take a risk—a calculated risk, but still a risk.

They too have an amygdala. But it worked just as hard to reject FALSE BAD NEWS as we work to reject FALSE GOOD NEWS. Or maybe they really are less afraid. "Numerous studies have been performed where researchers have used *deep lesioning* (procedure where a thin wire is inserted into the brain to remove or terminate a part of the brain) to remove the amygdala of rats. After this procedure, the rats were said to have no fear of anything, even cats. The removal of the amygdala had taken away the rats' memory of fear; therefore the rats did not fear anything!" www.TheBrainMadeSimple.com .

The retirement approach you will read about in this book is meant to protect against several real fears, so that your F.E.A.R. Factor is in balance:

- Running out of money as we live longer lives
- Medical bankruptcy
- Failure to leave a legacy
- Stock market risk
- Heavy taxation

Unfortunately, the approach you will learn about in this book has its hazards. There are real cautions you must understand. But, if you do, the potential for an ideal retirement increases mightily. Don't have an amygdala hijack. Think for yourself.

3. Danger is lurking from every naysayer who will dissuade you from creating a system that is truly guaranteed to insure your future income.

They will ignorantly spout bad news about products and services that go against the "herd mentality," and you will get too scared to make a move.

Wow. I got carried away there, didn't I? Well, forgive me, but I do get frustrated. You see, I have a very particular emphasis on helping my clients and it is contrary to what many planners, the financial press, and the hosts of financial TV shows may have to say.

F.E.A.R., once again stands for

F=False: It's not true or is a one-sided version of the truth.
E=Evidence: It sounds right because it's backed up with self-serving facts or is spouted by so-called experts, so it must be true.
A=Affecting: It has an impact; in our case negative.
R=Retirement: The effect is on your retirement planning, investing, and eventually your lifestyle.

With all the false or self-serving information out there, I do get frustrated for you more than for myself.

By RONALD GELOK, with Adriane Berg

My approach to retirement planning turns traditional planning on its head:

- ➢ I look at taxes first; I want you to spend time on saving them.
- ➢ I like products created by insurance companies that offer a system.
- ➢ I don't believe in your owning anything, I mean anything, you can't understand.
- ➢ I do believe that retirement planning is not that complicated.
  - Know your monthly income needs.
  - Determine if your guaranteed income covers them.
  - If not, let's get the income guarantees to cover the shortfall.
  - Make that income as tax-free as possible.
  - Cover healthcare surprises.

That's it.

Many times I come up with a system for a client that does all that, and the next thing you know their brother-in-law reads something negative about my suggestions from news reporters or bloggers, and they pull out. They insist on following the herd with just more stocks and bonds.

It doesn't trouble my practice because I am a wealth manager and can offer them services that are stock- and bond-related. But I am worried about this type of derailment for you. Don't let naysayers stop you from finishing this book and the 15 minutes of exercises that will change your future.

Please promise yourself that you will stay the course. If you do, I will make a promise to you. You can visit my office personally or have a Skype visit, and we will help you with any area in which you are stuck, whether you are a client or not. Fair?

Start dreaming big. Visit www.fearfactorthebook.com and get our hints and tips on answering the *7 Big Questions*.

Now, take a deep breath and discover the secret to the ideal retirement in less than 15 minutes.

By RONALD GELOK, with Adriane Berg

Chapter 2

How to Lead the Tax-Free Retirement Lifestyle

We cover: How a tax-free retirement lifestyle can be the same as putting 33% extra buying power in your pocket.

What you will discover:

➢ How taxable income, including distributions from pension and other plans are diminished by taxes.

➢ Tax-free lifestyle also means low state income tax living, low sales-tax living, estate and luxury tax, property tax.

➢ A map of different types of taxes in different states in the United States.

➢ Why prepaying tax may be the hidden secret of an ideal retirement.

What to do next:

Take a guesstimate as to your tax bracket after retirement. If you like DIY there are calculators at www.fearfactorthebook.com. If you want our help, visit that site and get your complimentary review.

No other retirement guide that I know of starts with an emphasis on tax savings. In fact, postretirement taxation is usually an afterthought. I know tax planning seems boring and like the cart before the horse.

Most people figure, gee, we're not going to have an income from a salary, so we're going to be in a much lower tax bracket. But what actually happens when we start to make withdrawals from our 401(k)s, 403(b)s, or other qualified plans? Taxes hit us then.

Look at it this way: you can increase your net worth, your income, your ability to spend, and your buying power, sometimes by as much as a third, just by doing the right tax planning.

If you could turn $100,000 a year into $133,000 a year with no extra risk, you would do so. That's the effect of good tax planning. But it does take diligence and a refusal to run with the herd.

By RONALD GELOK, with Adriane Berg

The ideal retirement is not just about what your gross income is; it's about what you get to keep and what you get to spend.

Maybe it's my background as a tax and estate attorney that makes me particularly sensitive to this, but there is a plethora of taxes that retirees are inundated with which they don't take into account: income taxes on distributions from retirement plans, capital gains taxes from the sale of investments, dividend income that's subject to tax, and the sometimes overwhelming property taxes.

If you don't take taxes into account and put strategies in place to deal with them, you're setting yourself up for failure.

Start by embracing the concept of the tax-free retirement lifestyle.

How can we immediately increase our spending power after retirement by as much as one-third by concentrating on our taxes?

If you start taking income from an IRA or a 401(k), those income distributions are subject to income tax at ordinary income tax rates, and that's both federal and, in the majority of states, state income taxes as well.

Let's also consider this: most people work to get to the point where they own their house free and clear in retirement, which also means there's no more mortgage interest deduction. And at that point the kids are through college. They're on their own (hopefully). There are no more deductions for dependents.

So, at the time in your life that deductions for dependents and mortgage interest are gone, withdrawals from retirement plans are subject to state and federal ordinary income taxes.

And a time comes when, even if you have enough income to live on, you are forced to take withdrawals from your qualified plans, and that gets taxed.

Required Minimum Distributions (RMDs) are the distributions that are mandated by law to begin following the April 1st after you have turned 70 1/2. There is a 50% penalty if you fail to pay, and you still owe the tax.

By RONALD GELOK, with Adriane Berg

As you go through your 70s and beyond, the percentage of your retirement portfolio in an IRA, 403(b), 401(k), or other qualified plan that must be distributed increases. What's really startling to me is people are told they shouldn't take any money out of their retirement accounts in their 60s because they may be subject to income tax, without taking into consideration that income tax rates in the future may be significantly higher than they are today.

Required Minimum Distribution

Table 4: Required Minimum Distributions

Age	Factor	Required Minimum Distribution
70	27.4	3.65%
71	26.5	3.77%
72	25.6	3.91%
73	24.7	4.05%
74	23.8	4.20%
75	22.9	4.37%
76	22.0	4.55%
77	21.2	4.72%
78	20.3	4.93%
79	19.5	5.13%

F.E.A.R. Factor and the RMD

Although we will explore this more in later chapters, here is an example of False Evidence Affecting Retirement. We are primed to believe that tax deferral is to our benefit all the time, because if you pay tax on growth and invest the remainder, there is less to grow.

Sounds right.

Consider that you will have to pay a tax on the entire growth one day. That will come when you are least able to pay. So maybe, just maybe, you are better off paying the tax, having a bit less to invest, and then letting it grow tax-free from then on. Hmm, just maybe.

How would you know which is right for you?

By RONALD GELOK, with Adriane Berg

It just takes some calculations and a mindset not to run with the herd.

If you like DIY there are some calculators to use. Visit www.fearfactorthebook.com . If you want our help, you visit that site and get your complimentary review.

A Note From Adriane

To Move or Not to Move? That Is the Question: How to Save Money, Taxes, and Maybe Your Life

I was given a wonderful compliment the other day. I explained to my friend that I was looking for an inexpensive second home out west where my kids live. "One day," I told her, "I might end up living there full-time. If I need more space, I can always sell the place and move to something a little bigger." She replied, "I wouldn't believe most of my friends when they say they are willing to move in later life. But I believe you." I felt complimented that she thought I was the rare case, flexible enough to move at any age and not be stuck in one place.

Many of us, regardless of our wealth or lack of it, find ourselves inflexible when it comes to moving. That's just fine if you have plenty of capital to pay your heating bills, do the maintenance older homes demand, are near family, and have no need financially or socially to move. In that case, just skip this part.

But, if your home is a drag on you in any way, let me inspire you to let go.

For many people, more than 30% of their postretirement income goes to property upkeep, mortgage, insurance, landscaping, and other aspects of their home. Yet they cling to an old lifestyle that did work in the past but may not allow them to thrive as they age.

There are many reasons to move, but it does take nerve and flexibility. One of those reasons is taxation. For example, Ron is licensed in the state of Nevada. That is also one of the states where I'm looking at property. This is a no-income-tax state; it is also a good state for people who have assets like company stock and might have a high capital gain. As you can see from the maps in this book, you can control your level of taxation partly by where you reside. Of course, taxation is just a small part of where you choose to live.

By RONALD GELOK, with Adriane Berg

Some places are particularly suited to an active retirement lifestyle. Many places in the West and Southwest have large numbers of active communities with sports, clubs, hiking, and many other types of physical and social activity at your doorstep. Then there are college towns, which might nurture your desire for lifelong learning. Still other locations bill themselves as walkable communities, which are particularly friendly to older adults.

I spent two years working with the Legislature and Mental Health Association of Rockland County, New York, and the AARP to study and institute changes for their aging population. It's a wonderful pent-urban place to live.

You can find these life-affirming places throughout the United States. I also work with the American Mexican Retirement Association, www.AMAR.org.mx . Many of us are looking at second and even first homes abroad.

Retirement, longevity, and the income gap have shaken up our view of where and how we should be living after retirement. Getting rid of the burdens of high property taxes, heating bills, maintenance, and other home-related expenses might be all you need to close that gap and not go through any machinations, take any risks, or create any stress in your life.

I talk a lot about taking lemons and making lemonade. It is something I have done all of my life, starting at a young age. I assure you that setbacks can become breakthroughs if you let them. Where you live is one centerpiece of your life of great importance. If you are forced by circumstance to move or if you choose to close the income gap by moving, you must regard this as a benefit, not a failure. The new possibilities for your life, the ability to meet new people, to enter new worlds, to free yourself of your past, and to renew your future becomes easy when you do that one hard thing—move.

Perhaps it seems odd to address this fundamental lifestyle question in a chapter on taxation. I placed this material here deliberately. I hope you will start making connections between the details of financial planning and the big broad patterns of your life. When we talk about a holistic approach to retirement, it must start with the way you think about your future. One feature of moving is tax savings. Of course, it is only one and perhaps the least significant in making your choice. But it is part of the mix.

By RONALD GELOK, with Adriane Berg

If you use a planner other than us (hope not), use a retirement planner who works exclusively with retirees and preretirees.

Planners that specialize in helping you "accumulate" wealth while you are young may not understand how to "decumulate" your assets for lifelong income after retirement. They don't care much about taxes; all they want to do is defer payment (easy to do in a traditional 401(k) or IRA.) When it comes to retirement, you need an advisor with a different mindset and set of skills.

Here's an analogy to healthcare. We have a general practitioner, let's say, that keeps us on an even keel when we're younger. But then as we get older, we look to geriatricians, people who are specialists in the older-age body and mind. Yet we don't do that with our financial planners.

When I was a kid, we had a family doctor. The family doctor made house calls. Today it seems that every doctor is a specialist. It seems almost every attorney is a specialist. Yet the mistake that a lot of people make is dealing with financial generalists when it comes to the most important phase of their life, retirement, where the name of the game is to make sure that your money lasts at as long as you do and beyond.

When we're in the accumulation stage, the growth stage, we're looking for somebody who might be a wealth manager or a broker who is concentrating only on growth. We don't realize that we may need a different kind of specialist at the time of our life when we need to make distributions.

Uh-oh, you feel bad leaving your advisor—what to do?

Then don't. You have a podiatrist and a GP, right? You don't feel bad about that. Some planners and advisors specialize in certain approaches. For example, we are money managers but specialize in creating tax-free retirement income systems for clients. There is nothing wrong with using each for their expertise.

Other taxes

Now, of course, we have other kinds of taxes besides RMD income taxes that you need to think about in connection with retirement.

By RONALD GELOK, with Adriane Berg

Property taxes: Property taxes, particularly in the Northeast, can take up a significant portion of a retiree's income. My birth state of New Jersey is one of the most notoriously high tax states. That's why, as Adriane wrote, a lot of people do think about retiring in other parts of the country, simply because they are aware of the state property and income tax issues.

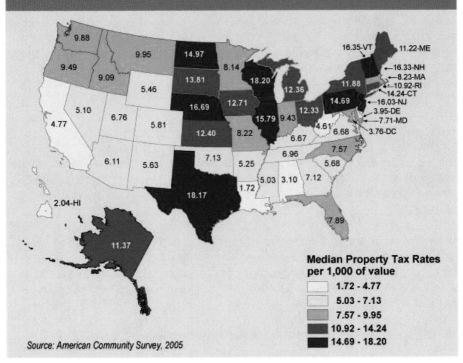

Median Real Estate Tax Rates per 1,000 of Value

Source: American Community Survey, 2005

Median Property Tax Rates per 1,000 of value
- 1.72 - 4.77
- 5.03 - 7.13
- 7.57 - 9.95
- 10.92 - 14.24
- 14.69 - 18.20

Dividends: Dividend income is subject to regular, normal state income taxes.

By RONALD GELOK, with Adriane Berg

Top State Income Tax Rates
Highest Statutory Marginal Income Rate By State, Tax Year 2011
www.TaxFoundation.org

Capital gains tax: If you sell an investment at a profit, you can run into state capital gains rates, as well as federal.

Now, depending on what your overall level of income is, your federal capital gains tax rate is either going to be 15% or 20%. And, in many states—New Jersey for example—you have an additional state capital gains tax rate of 7%.

Washington State Budget & Policy Center | budgetandpolicy.org

42 States Tax Capital Gains

31 states tax capital gains at rates higher than
the 5 percent rate proposed in Washington

States that tax capital gains (42)

States that do not tax capital gains (8)

Source: Budget & Policy Center analysis of Federation of Tax Administrators data

State estate tax: In New Jersey, for example, estates over $675,000 are subject to state estate taxes when money passes to the next generation. In New York, estates over $1 million are subject to state estate taxes. Then, almost to add insult to injury, in New Jersey if you leave money to nonlineal descendants such as nieces and nephews, you then run into an additional 15% state inheritance tax.

So there are all kinds of taxes that can be minimized or avoided through proper planning.

By RONALD GELOK, with Adriane Berg

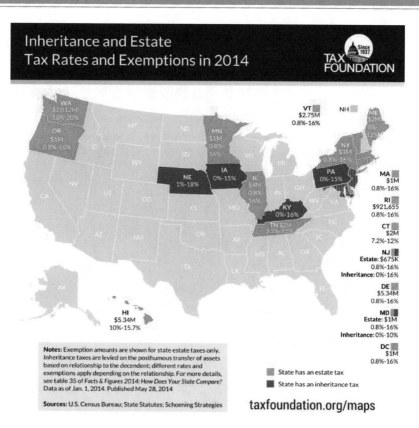

Inheritance and Estate
Tax Rates and Exemptions in 2014

TAX FOUNDATION
Since 1937

Notes: Exemption amounts are shown for state estate taxes only. Inheritance taxes are levied on the posthumous transfer of assets based on relationship to the decendent; different rates and exemptions apply depending on the relationship. For more details, see table 35 of *Facts & Figures 2014: How Does Your State Compare?* Data as of Jan. 1, 2014. Published May 28, 2014

Sources: U.S. Census Bureau; State Statutes; Schoening Strategies

State has an estate tax
State has an inheritance tax

taxfoundation.org/maps

Sales tax: We can pay from 3% to 10% sales tax at the register. That's quite a fee. Now restaurants and even some movies have a sales tax.

By RONALD GELOK, with Adriane Berg

Sales Tax: Combined State and Average Local Rates
Tax Year 2011
www.TaxFoundation.org

Luxury tax: Some states charge a special tax on luxury cars or luxury items in an estate.

Federal estate tax: As of January 2013, the federal estate tax was not imposed on estates under $5,250,000. This has been indexed to inflation so that in 2014 the number is $5,340,000. (Government policymakers have proposed dropping the threshold to $3,500,000 in 2018. Beyond that amount a tax of 40% is imposed. Feel exempt? Keep in mind that the rate has changed 12 times in 15 years and was almost down to a $1,000 exclusion. So who knows ?

Most asset-allocation plans or so-called retirement plans overlook these tax-related money bleeders.

Anybody can make a plan. You can get a do-it-yourself plan from Internet websites, or you can walk into a lot of financial planning firms and get plans that are essentially boilerplate, software-driven plans that really are not solutions or strategies. They're just glorified asset-allocation models.

What you must strive to do is identify what's the income-generating capacity of your assets and how you can structure those assets in such a way as to maximize them. This includes knowing how to make your income tax-advantaged or even tax-free so you know how much you can count on every month for the rest of your life.

Did you know it is okay to save taxes where you can? A famous judge said so.

Many people are afraid to save taxes—they see it as unpatriotic or think tax avoidance will get them in trouble. For those who may feel this way, there's a quote I like to cite from the famous judge Learned Hand.

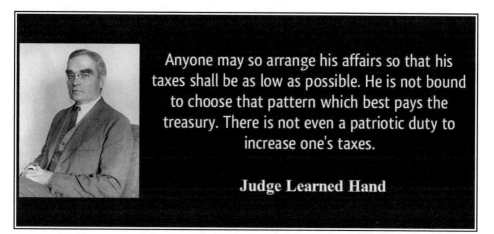

Anyone may so arrange his affairs so that his taxes shall be as low as possible. He is not bound to choose that pattern which best pays the treasury. There is not even a patriotic duty to increase one's taxes.

Judge Learned Hand

Judge Hand, continued: *"Over and over again the courts have said that there is nothing sinister in so arranging affairs as to keep taxes as low as possible. Everyone does it, rich and poor alike, and all do right for nobody owes any public duty to pay more than the law demands."*

It's very surprising that we have a judge telling us it's our duty to try to save taxes. It's not our duty to pay more than we should.

You don't want to run out of money before you run out of breath. You want to optimize your quality of life in retirement, and that's really what it's all about.

Our clients are very smart people. They have excelled in their chosen careers, but they're smart enough to know that there are areas where they could use a little help.

By RONALD GELOK, with Adriane Berg

Some of the solutions that we often suggest to clients for the ideal retirement start with this interesting concept:

Insurance for your wealth!

Now, I don't mean an insurance policy, although that will enter the picture in later chapters. I mean the concept of transferring the risk of running out of money so that you save taxes, or be largely tax-free, and protect against loss with a monthly check that covers the expenses of your ideal retirement.

Nobody goes through retirement driving around without car insurance. Nobody goes through retirement by canceling their homeowner's insurance. And nobody goes through retirement canceling their health insurance. Our premise is that it may actually make some sense to take a portion of retirement savings and position it in a tax-free guaranteed way—insure it, if you will.

Structure your assets in such a way as to generate tax-free distributions when your RMD date rolls around. Structure things in such a way as to participate in the upside of certain market indices like the S&P 500 offer and still limit the downside.

15 Minutes of Custom Planning: A Preview

It's back to what I said earlier. Sometimes we don't know what we don't know, and our job is not only to plan for our clients, but to educate our clients, bring them up to speed, and give them a whole new set of skills and strategies.

We are not afraid to look at offerings from insurance companies just because some offerings might not be desirable in our view.

Here we go retraining our thinking.

I am afraid to count how many times in this book I apologize for how the words *annuity* and even *insurance* are used to confuse you. It's such a turnoff that I worry you will just stop reading. Please don't. I have amazing things for you to discover about both annuities and insurance, but what I mean by those words is not what you think. The type of annuity and the types of insurance you are against, I am against, too.

By RONALD GELOK, with Adriane Berg

I know that one area of F.E.A.R., False Evidence Affecting Retirement, is that anything called an annuity is bad. You must understand that **any** savings program that can provide guaranteed income and is offered by an insurance company is usually categorized as an annuity account. But all annuity accounts are not created equally. There are some we would not want to touch with a ten-foot pole. There are a handful that are ideal for producing guaranteed, tax-free income at retirement without giving up control of principal.

We also often structure another type of system using something known as Indexed Universal Life Insurance (IULI), also from an insurance company, to grow money free from current taxes and create spendable distributions that are not subject to income taxes.

Most of us think we know what insurance companies have to offer, but we don't know about these offerings.

Why not? Let's be honest, there is a prejudice, not entirely undeserved, against insurance companies. With the know-how you will receive in upcoming chapters, you will see how to create and structure a system more to your benefit as opposed to the benefit of the company.

But you again have to be open to planning with something new, something the herd does not embrace. You will have to close your ears to blanket criticism of anything that comes from an insurance company. If you are willing to do so, it will take 15 minutes to get you

1. Tax-free income
2. Growth when stock indices rise
3. Guarantees against loss if the stock market tanks
4. Healthcare coverage for long-term care without paying for a long-term care policy
5. Coverage with a death benefit for a surviving spouse or other heir

By RONALD GELOK, with Adriane Berg

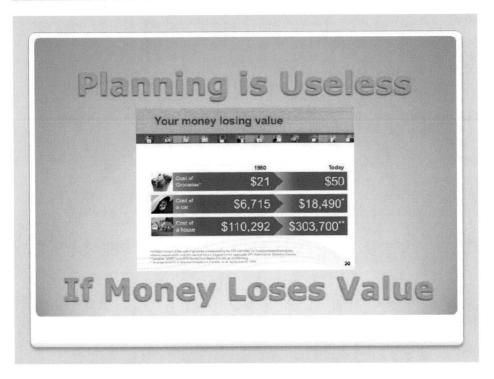

If you have paid attention, these are the features that solve the retirement soft spots revealed when you reviewed the **7 Big Questions** in Chapter 1. These are solutions to the toughest retirement issues.

Now, you understand that in the long run, taxes of all types are lifestyle killers. Concentrate on your post-retirement tax status. If you like DIY, there are some calculators to use at www.fearfactorthebook.com . If you want our help, visit that site and get your complimentary review. Get a good idea of the tax bite when you start to take money from your qualified plans.

Next, I will show you how to live an enhanced tax-free lifestyle by creating a system (not just a plan) in only 15 minutes that's right for you.

Chapter 3

What's the Difference between a Plan and a System?

We cover: A plan is what most people think about when it comes to retirement; that's why so few people actually plan for retirement. Not only is it tedious, scary, and unfocused, but it often makes you face questions that you have a very hard time answering. A system answers the question of how much you will have to live on. Then it's easier to make choices on how you want to live.

You will discover:

➢ How to answer planners when they ask: Where would you like to live? What lifestyle do you envision after retirement? Not only are these difficult to answer, but couples may have different answers, and everyone changes their answers a year or two or more after retirement. Yet almost every retirement plan asks you how much you need to live in retirement. How should you know?

➢ The best answer: "I'll live on the maximum amount of money I possibly can without running out before I leave this earth."

➢ Why people don't plan for retirement. No plan can help you see into the future. That's why you are likely to spend more time planning your vacation than planning your retirement. It's not because you're bad, it's because you're not clairvoyant.

➢ With a system, we look at what you have today and maximize it as much as we possibly can. One essential strategy is to eliminate taxation.

What to do next:

➢ The first part of creating our system is determining the "income gap," or the gap between what's needed to live your ideal retirement lifestyle and what you have in fixed guaranteed income. Visit www.fearfactorthebook.com to determine your income gap.

➢ Review the elements of your ideal retirement at www.fearfactorthebook.com

By RONALD GELOK, with Adriane Berg

Why are we so afraid to plan? And why do we notoriously fail to plan for our retirement?

Of course, we all want to have clarity and certainty about what our retirement will be like. Perhaps we've had a bad experience or two with a financial advisor; we've been asked to answer all kinds of questions about where we want to live and what we see in our future. The questions are vague. We tend to sensor ourselves until we know how much money we will have in retirement. We ask ourselves which comes first, the dream or the money to pay for the dream?

Eventually, we get so frustrated that we turn on the TV and watch *The Big Bang Theory*, HGTV, or the World Poker Tour and forget about retirement planning.

To no avail. The need to plan creeps up on us another day. I can't let you off the hook either. Visit www.fearfactorthebook.com to answer the **7 Big Questions** we asked in Chapter 1, if you haven't already.

I bet you're still struggling with them if the question of "Will I be able to afford it?" restricts your desires. I almost have to laugh at websites that offer a calculator that purports to tell you how much net worth you're going to need and how much income you're going to need based on what you are currently spending. That's just not a system. It is not helpful. In fact, the questions themselves can invoke fear.

If the DIY websites don't help, a financial salesperson may actually harm.

Anybody can talk a good game. What happens to a lot of people is they end up dealing with "advisors" who have great personalities and who are great salespeople but who never put together any kind of written roadmap to follow. My goal is not that you have a financial plan, which is just a piece of paper with boilerplate spread sheets, but a system that covers THE FOUR CENTRAL RETIREMENT ISSUES:

1. Tax-Free Income
2. Stock Market Volatility Protection
3. Inheritance
4. Catastrophic Illness

By RONALD GELOK, with Adriane Berg

Preretirees come into my office all the time with 100-page-long plans that don't help them do what they want to do or know what they want to know.

Our philosophy is a little bit different. Our philosophy is that you need a system. We need to take a look at the tax character of your assets, and we need to put together a plan to optimize your income. We need to put a system in place that includes answers to these questions:

Where: From where will you take money after retirement?
When: When are you going to start making withdrawals?
How: How will you spend and enjoy the money?

Clients leave our office with a sense of clarity and peace of mind about their future. At least that's what they report back to me. That's why we're so system-oriented as opposed to boilerplate plan-oriented.

I will start a meeting by asking, "What's the most important problem that you would like us to help you solve?" Oftentimes the problem I'll hear about is a gap between what's coming in through fixed income like a pension and Social Security or just Social Security, and the amount of expenses.

This gap is created when a plan calls for asset allocation and then makes assumptions on how much income will be earned by investing assets according to that allocation. Even with a conservative estimate, stock markets are not controlled by plans; there are no guarantees.

The Income Gap

The first part of creating our system is determining the income gap, the gap between what's needed to live your ideal retirement lifestyle and what you have in fixed guaranteed income.

Clients confess to me all the time, "You know what, Ron? I shouldn't say this, but I'm really scared to death. I've got X amount of dollars in the 401(k), and this is supposed to last me and my spouse for the next 30 years."

We take a look at the income-generating capacity of a person's assets, but we do much more than that. We look at incorporating the idea of guarantees. If we just leave everything at risk and we try to diversify for protection, in the uncertain world that we live in today, that's not good enough.

By RONALD GELOK, with Adriane Berg

Most plans will assume 6% growth for you a year and a withdrawal rate of 4%. (This is changing to only 3.5% in many standard plans, as 4% is often a formula to outlive your money.) Then you get a spreadsheet of how much you have to live on. But a plan never guarantees you are going to get that 6% or 10% or whatever percentage it assumes.

Yet, asset allocation and diversification seems to be the herd mentality answer to every risk question. Either that or stay out of the stock market and earn pennies on the dollar.

That's why it's so important to think outside the box and intelligently use select offerings from insurance companies to help bridge the income gap.

Riders the Key to the System

I just checked, there are over 30 places in this book that I mention the word 'rider.' A rider is a clause in a contract that is added to the basic terms, or policy or annuity agreement. Riders differ from company to company, cost money or are free, serve your purpose or do not.

It is the use of the correct riders for you that will make the difference between an "ideal" and a "so-so" retirement financial system. Before we go any further, here is a list of some of the more popular riders we will refer to throughout this book:

a. **Lifetime income benefit riders**: These riders allow for a specific rate of guaranteed growth for purposes of meeting future income needs. For example, one popular version of this rider allows for a 6.5% growth rate for 15 years and will also allow for lifetime income withdrawals at rates of 4 to 6% guaranteed for life. A typical cost might be 0.75% per year, but we also have access to some companies that offer lifetime income benefit riders at zero cost.

b. **Long-term care riders**: A long-term care rider can allow for acceleration of policy benefits to pay for long–term care. Costs range from free to 0.95% per year.

c. **Nursing home riders**: A nursing home rider allows for greater access to policy benefits in the event of a nursing home stay. Many companies will offer this benefit at no additional cost.

d. **Terminal illness riders**: A terminal illness rider allows for withdrawal of policy values on a penalty-free basis in the event of a diagnosis of a terminal illness. Costs range from free to 0.50% per year.

e. **Chronic illness riders**: An example of this type of rider is a rider that allows policy benefits to be accessed rapidly to pay for the expenses of a chronic illness. Costs range from free to 1.0% per year.

f. **"Income-doubler" riders**: An "income-doubler" rider typically allows for guaranteed income benefits under a policy to be doubled in the event of a need for home health care, assisted living, nursing home care, or diagnosis of a cognitive impairment. Costs range from 0.10% to 1.0% per year.

No Guarantees

It is these riders that can move our retirement income from non-guaranteed to guaranteed.

A fundamental of wealth management is the concept that assets get positioned differently in different buckets, each with different purposes. One bucket might be income now. Another bucket might be income later. One bucket might be tax-free growth and tax-free income down the road.

When you are postretirement the "income now" bucket must be guaranteed, if you want to live worry-free. But you'll never hear a wealth manager talk in terms of guarantees. In fact, under certain circumstances it's unethical to do so and maybe even a violation of the law. When securities are being used, there are no guarantees. When we look at offerings from insurance companies, that's where we can get a guaranteed component into the mix.

Just to give you an example, let's suppose a person says, "I'm 62 years old. I want to figure out what to do with this 401(k) rollover, and

By RONALD GELOK, with Adriane Berg

I don't think I'm going to need income from this particular bucket or this particular account until age 70." Well, we can go to a number of top-rated insurance companies, and we can look at fixed annuity accounts that offer index linked interest, so we've got some meaningful upside potential. (More about that later.)

We've got programs that lock in nice interest credits in the good years, avoid losses in the down years, and, at the same time, offer a rider to the system that gives a guarantee. Instead of assuming a 6% rate, you get a guarantee that the money is compounding along at 6 to 6.5% per year specifically for the purpose of creating a guaranteed income stream for life that you take at age 70 or beyond.

We can also include guarantees of a floor on the downside with features that prevent a loss if the market goes down and yet allow you to participate in the upside of a good market.

These are real solutions to some of the central issues of retirement. As I explained, I am a wealth manager. I manage portfolios through asset allocation with no guarantees. Yet I have never seen so much peace of mind in my clients than when they have system-based guarantees.

In a growth scenario for younger people, wealth management with asset allocation might be ideal. If there is a big surge or big bubble in the stock market, they're going to participate 100%. But in the second stage of your life where you may be decumulating and using your money, you may find it much more important to have guarantees against loss than the highest upside potential.

Only then are you really protected and can use other assets to take a risk, pay for legacy and gifting, and feel free to live the ideal retirement.

Yes Guarantees

There are two offerings from insurance companies to consider:

Fixed indexed annuities (FIAs) can provide a guaranteed rate of growth. FIAs can be owned in an IRA whether you choose to buy with taxable or after-tax dollars in a qualified plan, or they may be purchased after you have taken money from a qualified plan and paid the tax.

The income credited to you is linked to the performance of a stock market index, but a definite amount of income is guaranteed. Usually that amount is 6, 6.5, or 7%. Now if you use the 4% annual withdrawal rule, you will never run out of money. These guarantees require that you add a rider to your annuity called a guaranteed lifetime income benefit rider.

For example, with a lifetime income benefit rider guaranteeing 6% interest, compounded, money will double in 12 years, regardless of stock market volatility.

Indexed Universal Life Insurance (IUL) is the original version of an insurance product that came on the scene in 1995. It wasn't such a great choice then for many reasons, but the new design can create the type of system that works to solve all four central issues of retirement.

Types of Guarantees

Guarantees to protect principal:

The rate of interest is tied to the performance of an external market index such as the S&P 500 index. Now, granted, there may be some caps on the upside earnings, but once your annual credit is posted to your account, that's yours to keep. If the following year is a 2008, and you just had a double-digit interest credit, for example, the year before, you're not giving back any of what you just earned the prior year.

This is astounding to people who say, "You mean to tell me there are vehicles out there that allow me to have my principal protected against loss, and still have upside potential? I keep what I make in good years, I avoid losses in down years, and I have lifetime income guarantees besides?" I'm saying, "Yes, absolutely yes."

Death benefit: You have death benefit insurance as well, which pays your beneficiary. You can also structure it to avoid probate.

Tax-free income: You can borrow your accumulated cash value tax-free to add to income. (More about that in other chapters.)

Tax-deferred income: Your income is credited tax-deferred and grows tax-deferred like an IRA. If you don't want the tax-free loan, your account is growing and you can withdraw funds at will and pay an income tax.

Flexible contribution and withdrawal rules: You can make contributions from any funds, not just earned income; you can take out money or leave it in. Of course, this is not a qualified plan, so there is no RMD. There is no age limit for contribution or withdrawal either.

Does not affect tax on Social Security: Yes, Social Security may be taxable, depending on your income from other sources. Distributions from qualified plans may affect your Social Security. Distributions from IULI will not be counted in determining the Social Security tax.

F.E.A.R. Factor at Work; Who Made *Annuity* and *Insurance* Dirty Words?

When I mention *annuity* or *insurance* to people, it creates a certain amount of confusion because there are just so many misconceptions about annuities and insurance-based products.

There are some annuities that are created by trading a lump sum for a stream of guaranteed income for life or for a number of years, and the investor relinquishes the lump sum. **You lose control of that lump sum.**

Sure, you have the income, but if you step off a curb and get hit by a bus, the income stops. The insurance company keeps the money.

That's nothing like the retirement annuities we are talking about in this book. Yet people close their minds to systems with ideal features just because they use the word *annuity*. The F.E.A.R. Factor kicks in.

This happens to everyone. Even me. In writing that an immediate annuity is not my cup of tea, I was reminded by a colleague that many older adults get peace of mind with an immediate annuity guaranteed for a term of years. If they pass away before the term is up, the income goes to an heir. Not my type of annuity, but under the correct circumstance even immediate annuities work for some.

The other end of the spectrum is a securities product known as a variable annuity, which can have ridiculously, in my opinion, high fees and expenses, sometimes 3.5% per year or more. We're not recommending that to you either.

By RONALD GELOK, with Adriane Berg

Then, in the middle space is what's known as the fixed annuity account. Interest rates are so low that watching your nest egg grow is like watching grass grow. You might be getting a little bit better interest rate than a certificate of deposit, but I don't want them either.

So much negativity surrounds immediate, fixed, and variable annuities that it's hard to use the word *annuity* and not get a negative reaction.

All I ask is that you pay attention, stay focused, and not have a knee-jerk reaction based on false evidence from naysayers who know half the story of annuities.

True, there are some annuity programs that have obscene fees and expenses, and we avoid those like the plague. I'll tell you, honestly, for every 100 annuity contracts that I review, I'd say 98 of them, 99 of them, I'll throw in the garbage because they're written in favor of the insurance company, in my opinion, and not the consumer. But there are a handful of products that are absolutely ideal for solving the income gap. Yet I expect pushback solely because the herd does not like the word *annuity*. We buy into the negatives as gospel and succumb to the F.E.A.R. Factor.

Think again.

We have reviewed the type of annuity we are NOT suggesting. So what are we suggesting?

A Note From Adriane

Examples of How Insurance Contracts Create an Income Stream

I'm terrible at math. Yes, this is an occupational hazard for someone like me who is a financial journalist and writer. It doesn't help much in my marketing career either. So I have devised a way to understand the numbers I need in my life. I find that by struggling with my understanding, I can explain it better to you. Here's another example of making lemonade out of lemons.

I found myself at this stage of the book very interested in getting the numbers that might apply under different circumstances. So, I asked Patricia Nealy, a member of the Gelok team, to give me some hypotheticals. She sent me lots of numbers, just like you'll get when you get your printouts of various annuities or universal life insurance policies or income riders. Phooey, how head-breaking for the right-brained among us. So, I'm going to explain two examples to you in the same way that I developed my understanding for myself.

First let's look at a couple both age 66. They have $500,000 for the purpose of filling their income gap and maximizing their nest egg. The insurance company offers a bonus when they sign up of 5% of their investment, so they actually start with $525,000. The payout calculation will be for both their lives so that when one passes on, the other of the couple keeps getting income. They will also defer payments for one year. This means they will not be taking anything out until they are 67 years old. They plan to make withdrawals at the rate of 4.2% of their nest egg every year. This is in keeping with the usual suggestion of taking 4% out to live on from your retirement savings.

They also want to cover the problem of long-term care, as best they can. They have added an Income Doubler Rider for Long Term Care. If they cannot do certain activities of daily living like bathing, feeding, toileting, or moving or have dementia, and the waiting period has elapsed (anywhere from one to three years depending on the contract), they get much more in income than if they had no rider. You will see how much more when you compare the fifth column payment to the normal guaranteed monthly payment.

Years Deferred	Age	Income Account Value	Guaranteed Annual Payment	Income Doubler LTC Rider Payment
1	67	$559,125	$23,483	$23,783
2	68	$595,468	$25,605	$25,605
3	69	$634,173	$27,903	$41,855
4	70	$675,394	$30,392	$45,589
5	71	$719,295	$32,227	$49,091
6	72	$766,049	$35,238	$52,857
7	73	$815,042	$37,936	$56,905
8	74	$868,872	$40,837	$61,255
9	75	$925,349	$43,954	$65,931
10	76	$985,497	$47,303	$70,955
11	77	$1,049,554	$50,903	$76,355
12	78	$1,117,775	$54,771	$82,156
13	79	$1,190,430	$58,926	$88,389
14	80	$1,267,808	$63,390	$95,085
15	81	$1,350,216	$67,510	$101,266
16	82	$1,437,980	$71,889	$107,848
17	83	$1,531,449	$76,572	$114,858
18	84	$1,630,993	$81,549	$122,324
19	85	$1,737008	$86,850	$130,275
20	86	$1,849,913	$92,495	$138,743

By RONALD GELOK, with Adriane Berg

An Income Doubler LTC rider, and there are many names for the same thing, costs money. In this particular illustration a .85% annual fee is withdrawn from the contract value.

They also could choose a rider called lifetime income benefit rider, which works as follows.

Following a single premium payment (in this illustration, $500,000), you can begin making income payment withdrawals for life. The longer you choose to defer the taking of the withdrawals, the larger the withdrawal will be, starting at $2,599 per month immediately to $8,841 per month if you wait for 25 years before making withdrawals.

Beginning of Year to Start Income Withdrawals	Attained Age	Premium Amount	Benefit Base Bonus	Beginning of Year Benefit Base	Income Withdrawal Percentage	Annual Income Withdrawal Amount	Monthly Income Withdrawal Amount
1	66	$500,000	50,000	550,000	N/A	N/A	N/A
2	67	$0	0	585,750	N/A	N/A	N/A
3	68	$0	0	623,824	5.00%	$31,191	$2,599
4	69	$0	0	664,372	5.00%	$33,219	$2,768
5	70	$0	0	707,556	5.50%	$38,916	$3,243
6	71	$0	0	753,548	5.50%	$41,445	$3,454
7	72	$0	0	802,528	5.50%	$44,139	$3,678
8	73	$0	0	854,693	5.50%	$47,008	$3,917
9	74	$0	0	910,248	5.50%	$50,064	$4,172
10	75	$0	0	969,414	6.00%	$58,165	$4,847
11	76	$0	0	1,032,426	6.00%	$61,946	$5,162
12	77	$0	0	1,099,533	6.00%	$65,972	$5,498
13	78	$0	0	1,171,003	6.00%	$70,260	$5,855
14	79	$0	0	1,247,118	6.00%	$74,827	$6,236
15	80	$0	0	1,328,181	6.50%	$86,332	$7,194
16	81	$0	0	1,414,513	6.50%	$91,943	$7,662
17	82	$0	0	1,414,513	6.50%	$91,943	$7,662
18	83	$0	0	1,414,513	6.50%	$91,943	$7,662
19	84	$0	0	1,414,513	6.50%	$91,943	$7,662
20	85	$0	0	1,414,513	7.00%	$99,016	$8,251
21	86	$0	0	1,414,513	7.00%	$99,016	$8,251
22	87	$0	0	1,414,513	7.00%	$99,016	$8,251
23	88	$0	0	1,414,513	7.00%	$99,016	$8,251
24	89	$0	0	1,414,513	7.00%	$99,016	$8,251
25	90	$0	0	1,414,513	7.50%	$106,088	$8,841

There are a variety of both annuities and insurance products that create our system.

There are fixed annuity accounts that offer **index-linked interest.** Their features differ from the types of annuities that we do not usually recommend:

➢ The full value of the account goes to your surviving spouse or to your kids or beneficiaries if you pass on.

By RONALD GELOK, with Adriane Berg

> You get lifetime income guarantees that don't require you trading away your lump sum or losing control. As we mentioned earlier, they earn usually 6, 6 ½, or 7% compounded.

> They offer increased income features that protect you financially in case of catastrophic illness.

If you have been following along, you have a notion of your ideal retirement, some idea of the costs, and you know if you have an income gap or other issues to solve.

Review the facts about your finances:

> Where you would like to live
> When do you want to retire
> Whether you're going to be working a little in retirement, which is called the "new retirement" or "rehirement"
> If you want to travel, leave a legacy, start a new business . . . and all the wonderful things that boomers think about when they think about this extra 30, 40, 50 years that we have after retirement.

Imagine the ideal retirement once again. Is the vision getting clearer?

Now, you know we strive to create a system with income guarantees you can count on. When we go on to other chapters of this book, you'll be shocked at how much better you can live simply by having a system rather than a plan. But, like the word or not, to achieve this, your system will most likely include some sort of guaranteed annuity or insurance product.

Chapter 4

Why Is Tax-Free So Much Better Than Tax-Deferred?

We cover: Most Americans have been indoctrinated into the belief that paying taxes later rather than sooner is better for them. Initially this makes sense. If you are growing your wealth and don't have to pay taxes, then all of the gains are growing without diminishment by taxation. Over long periods of time, this does work out well. A time comes, however, anywhere from 10 to 5 years before retirement, when for many it no longer pays to defer taxes. It is better to pay the tax and invest tax-free from then on.

You will discover:

> ➤ How to determine when to convert your tax-deferred holdings into after-tax holdings

> ➤ How to withdraw funds from qualified accounts and pay the tax

> ➤ Ins and out of the Roth IRA

> ➤ Ins and outs of the system through indexed products

What to do next:

> ➤ Go to www.fearfactorthebook.com and you will find our calculator for a guesstimate of your future taxation. By the way, you will also get a good idea of the income you will have at retirement to determine a ballpark figure of your income gap, if any.

> ➤ If you have an insurance policy with cash value, check out our exchange article on www.fearfactorthebook.com.

Here I go again, harping on taxes. I just got you excited about a system that will guarantee against loss, allow participation in the stock market through certain indices, and fill your income gap. You are about ready to get over the F.E.A.R. of the words *annuity* and *insurance*; you are ready to create the system.

You are on a roll. Now I poke the balloon with the tax pin again. I'm sorry, but I must.

By RONALD GELOK, with Adriane Berg

I wish we lived in the world where we could get 6% or 7% yields on municipal bonds. Life would be easier, but we have to deal with the world the way it is, not the way we wish it was.

I can remember my grandmother having a conversation with my mother years ago where she said, "What should I do? There's one CD that'll pay me a 14% interest rate, and then there's a CD from another bank that'll pay me 13.875%, but they'll give me a toaster, an electric blanket, or a blender. Which one should I choose?"

Those were the days.

Tax-Free vs. Tax-Deferred

Let's focus on the difference between tax-free and tax-deferred. We may think we know what that means, but we may not realize what tax deferral does to us when we simply defer and don't pay taxes earlier.

I think we're all a little bit brainwashed to think that tax deferral is the be-all and end-all and a cure to all our retirement planning ills. We're told that we should sock away as much money as we possibly can in employer-sponsored plans because the money is growing free from current taxes.

Unfortunately, that premise is a false premise for many of us near retirement. It is based on the assumption that in retirement we'll be in a much lower tax bracket. When the time comes to take the money out, we'll be able to pay the tax with ease.

Will you be in a lower tax bracket at retirement? Let's find out right now.

Go to www.fearfactorthebook.com and you will find our calculator for a guesstimate of your future taxation. By the way, you will also get a good idea of the income you will have at retirement to determine a ballpark figure of your income gap, if any.

All planning is integrated. And all of it leads to clarity regarding the answers to your **Big 7 Questions**. This in turn leads to solutions through the correct system.

Will you have your current deductions, credits, and exclusions?

By RONALD GELOK, with Adriane Berg

When you're entering retirement you typically don't have deductions for mortgage interest any longer. You typically don't have deductions for dependent children anymore. And tax rates are not going lower in our society. Too much tax deferral can actually be like a pact with the devil. We're trading the right to defer current taxes during accumulation years for exposure to paying taxes under an unknown future tax rate, which could be much higher than we anticipated.

That's why my view is that tax-free is so much better than tax-deferred. My premise behind tax-free is that we create a system to accumulate wealth both free from current taxes and have income distributed to us tax-free for life, as well.

Required Minimum Distribution Revisited

Let's recall that tax deferral is just that—the tax must eventually be paid. We know exactly when. When we reach the April 1st after we turn 70 ½, we are forced to take distributions. Most of us haven't planned for the taxation at that point.

Do you have an employer-sponsored plan, a qualified plan, a 401(k), a 403(b), or a 457 plan? Did you ever wonder why a lot of these plans start with the number 4? It relates to the 400 section of the IRS code.

At 70 1/2, the RMD is only 3.65% of the prior December 31st value of your TOTAL deferred accounts. As you go through your 70s, the percentage that you're forced to take out increases. For example, at 72 it's approximately 4.2%. When you're in your 80s, it can be 6%. As you get older, you're forced to take out more money at unknown future tax rates.

At 70 1/2, for each $100,000 you have in an IRA, you have to take out $3,649.64. At 75, for each $100,000 of qualified plan money the RMD is up to $4,366.81. At 80, the RMD for each $100,000 of IRA or qualified plan money is now up to $5,347.59.

With increased longevity, we're very likely to be around to make those distributions for many decades, and we're paying taxes generally at a time that we really don't have the income for it.

Younger people often think that age brings anxiety over money. Some look at the money worries of older adults and call it "the depression mentality." I think that these concerns are real, not a syndrome or a fact of aging. We are living longer, our salary has stopped, our cost of living is up, our taxes are high, and we F.E.A.R. the loss of dignity that financial dependence can bring. No one wants to change their spending habits or lifestyle after 80 if they can help it.

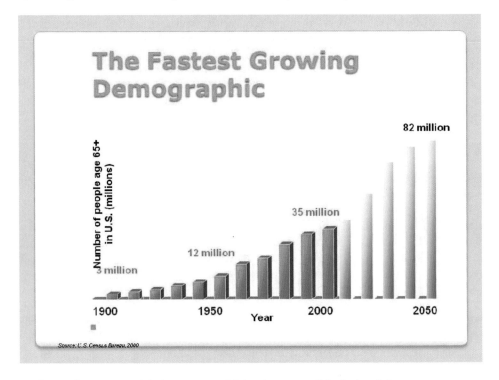

In fact, they say with boomers 60 is the new 30. I don't know; personally I think it's just that 60 is a new type of 60. And 70 will be a new type of 70. You may still be working. We may even be working until age 72, 73, 74, 75 because we want to and we like to, and the money is good.

But, we do stop eventually, and it's interesting that the deck is really stacked against us. The moment we stop working, usually in our early 70s if we stretch it, the distribution requirements go up. If we prepaid those taxes, if we were living tax-free by then, we probably would be much better off.

By RONALD GELOK, with Adriane Berg

A Note From Adriane

How do we determine when we need to move from a tax-deferred type of investing to a tax-free?

It's so important to work with advisors who have a skill set that includes both knowledge of the tax code and of how different financial products work in relation to taxation. If your retirement account is growing at 6% per year, it's going to double every 12 years. If it's growing at 7.2% per year, it's doubling every 10 years. And so somebody ultimately is going to pay the income tax on that money when it comes out.

To determine whether and when it's time to convert tax-deferred to tax-free, first determine the specific amount of money to come out of your qualified plans in your 60s, prior to 70 1/2 or whether you will wait until 70 1/2. If you do wait, will you distribute the RMD or more to cover the income gap?

You must also do Social Security income planning to determine the optimal age to start collecting Social Security so as to maximize lifetime benefits. Although there is no shortage of information on Social Security, I have found that one pamphlet explains it best. To get a complementary copy sent by mail, of "The Social Security Decisions, What, When, Who, How" just visit www.RonaldGelok/F.E.A.R.Factor and get your copy.

After completing your Social Security planning get an idea of total taxable income at retirement, tax bracket and calculate your retirement year's tax liability. If it's high, consider paying the tax now. Don't defer.

There are strategies that allow you to get money out of the qualified plans and go to an outside source to cover the tax liability so you can start investing tax-free from now on.

One of those strategies involves taking a **low** interest rate loan from an insurance company to cover the tax liability. If this is a strategy you may be interested in, you will want to come in and meet with us. We must explore how this tax-free alternative planning may work specifically for you. Of course, at its base, it requires that you do have an insurance policy that has already accumulated cash surrender value. We want to make very sure that your borrowing to pay taxes

By RONALD GELOK, with Adriane Berg

does not result in any lapse of policy and deprive you of your planned legacy. Therefore, I give you this information as an idea. But, as they say on TV, "Don't try this at home, work with a professional."

Get the calculators out.

Step into my online office. I will look at what we call "tax-free alternative planning" and compare the income you can expect under three different scenarios:

1) Staying in the traditional deferred plan and taking taxable income distributions
2) Paying taxes now and reinvesting in the same assets through a Roth IRA
3) Taking the money and buying into an indexed system with tax-free income and guarantees

With regard to the indexed system, the calculations will tell us whether it makes sense to get money out of an IRA, pay the tax to reposition assets in a program where we can grow our money free, but also pull out a tax-free income when we're ready to retire. This involves a little bit of thinking outside the box.

Here is a three-part comparison for a couple in the 35% tax bracket:

IRA vs Roth IRA vs Tax Free Plan--Summary

	Traditional IRA 7.70%	Roth IRA 7.70%	An Alternative Tax Free Plan 7.70%
Current Balance/Deposit/Premiums:	600,000	600,000	600,000
Re-allocation (Conversion) Taxes:	0	248,220 (41.37% T)	248,220 (41.37% T)
Income Benefits:	1,292,817	673,854	1,353,000
Total Taxes	534,838 (41.37% T)	0 (0% T)	0 (0% T)
Total Net Income/Tax Free Benefits:	757,978	673,854	1,353,000
Annual Income % to Monies Invested	6.83%	11.66%	11.66%
Total Income % to Monies Invested	126.33%	191.56%	384.62%
Family Benefits:	0	0	2,017,911
	757,978	673,854	3,370,911

By RONALD GELOK, with Adriane Berg

Graphical Summary of IRA vs Roth IRA vs Tax Free Plan

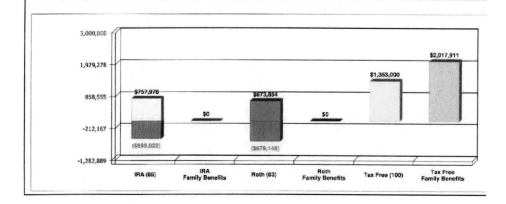

I know what you're thinking. I may not have the money to pay tax later, but I sure don't have the money to pay it now!

Aha, there are little-known strategies to get money out of the retirement plan and get the taxes covered using OPM, or other people's money. What if you could borrow the money to cover the taxes at an attractive interest rate?

We can look at several alternatives. They include borrowing against a cash value insurance policy as we discussed above, taking a loan from your qualified plan, or looking at your individual situation for sources of low-interest loans. (See above.)

Roth IRA

We've all heard of a Roth IRA, named after Senator William Roth of Delaware, who championed the code provision.

The Roth IRA in a nutshell:

1. Withdraw funds from a tax-deferred plan.
2. Pay the tax.
3. Transfer the after-tax funds to a Roth IRA or Roth 401(k).
4. Leave the funds in the Roth for five years.

After that any distributions you take out of your Roth IRA are not subject to income taxes.

By RONALD GELOK, with Adriane Berg

But you can't just wave a magic wand and switch your nest egg over to a tax-free Roth. First, there's a toll to pay, and that toll is what's known as the conversion tax, which is ordinary income tax on the amount that's being converted.

Let's say you convert a $500,000 traditional IRA or 401(k) to a Roth all at once. You could trigger federal income taxes at a 39.6% rate. Depending on what state you live in, you might trigger state income taxes at, say, an 8% rate. Also, if income is over $250,000 you may also trigger a 3.8% healthcare surtax. Over 50% of that 401(k) or traditional IRA is going to be wiped out in one fell swoop with taxes if someone gets overly aggressive in trying to convert all at once.

Sometimes it may make sense to look at gradual conversions. This is where we must think outside the box to determine whether making the switch is worth it in the long run.

Punch line: I believe that converting and paying a tax early is worth it if you will be in a higher tax bracket at retirement and PROVIDED you can continue to participate in the stock market with guarantees so you cannot lose in a recession. That means using your Roth with those pie chart assets for only some of your money and buying a system for the rest, at least enough to cover your income gap.

Oh, oh. This sounds expensive. First I pay a tax and then I buy an annuity or insurance product that charges fees. Not me.

A Note From Adriane

A Tip on Tax-Free Exchanges if You Have Insurance With Cash Value

You may have heard of tax-free exchanges in connection to real estate. But how can we take some of our tax-deferred dollars that are not in real estate and make a tax-free exchange to another asset, like an indexed system?

Here's an example. If you have an older, existing policy that has substantial cash surrender value, it may be in your best interest to do a tax-free exchange into a new policy. Mortality costs have dropped dramatically in recent years. Many times we can take an old paid-up policy, and do a tax-free exchange to another company, and

By RONALD GELOK, with Adriane Berg

substantially increase the death benefit with no additional out-of-pocket premium.

Also, there are new policies today that offer riders, which allow for accelerated payout of the death benefit to cover chronic illness, terminal illness, convalescent care, home health care, or nursing home care.

Sometimes a person no longer needs a life policy, and to surrender the policy can trigger an immediate tax liability. In those instances, a tax-free exchange to a tax-deferred annuity may be in your best interest. The bottom line is there is no "one-size-fits-all" right strategy when evaluating existing, older life policies. Ronald Gelok & Associates offers a valuable service in the form of a no-cost policy review of your existing policies.

Check out Ron's **Tax-Free Exchange** article on www.fearfactorthebook.com. And get your no obligation review.

F.E.A.R. Factor and the Boogeyman of Expenses

Often when we think life insurance, indexed or otherwise, we think expense, expense, expense. We're brainwashed to think that when you're young you get the least expensive term insurance you can find and, as soon as your mortgage is paid off and your kid's education is funded, get rid of it. What do you need that expense for anymore?

Our point of view is that provisions in the tax code are uniquely favorable toward insurance. We want to look at how to legally, morally, ethically take advantage of those tax code provisions to design an indexed life plan where we're not seeking to maximize the death benefit but are seeking to maximize the guaranteed income benefit.

When we minimize the death benefit, we also minimize the cost of insurance and optimize the ability of the system to grow your nest egg free from current taxes. Then YOU have the freedom to pull cash out of the policy tax-free.

How would we get cash out of an insurance policy tax-free? Through the device of the tax-free policy loan.

By RONALD GELOK, with Adriane Berg

F.E.A.R. Factor alert! This sounds scary and filled with fees. Put in my own money, borrow out my own money, and maybe pay interest to use my own money. Are you kidding me! What's the good of that?

I am asking you to cultivate a new point of view, for many of you a 180-degree change. It requires that you:

1) Concentrate on your taxes. They are not going to be made easier by deferral. Deferral comes back to bite you at some point in life.

2) Three to five years or so before retirement start to pay those taxes and invest for tax-free gain.

3) Then reposition for tax-free income. Yes, I like to get tax-free income by borrowing it out of the indexed policy.

Hang in there. I will explain.

Once you set up a tax-free lifestyle, keep it that way.

Under the IRC, loan proceeds are not taxable as income. No loan proceeds are taxable. For example, if you walk into the bank, you borrow money, and they give you a check, that's loan proceeds. That's not taxable income. If you have a properly structured tax-advantaged index life plan and you borrow from the insurance company, that's also tax-free loan proceeds.

Of course, you can always take out money up to the amount of premium you contributed. But then you pay a surrender charge. It's like breaking a CD before it's due; the bank charges for that. If you wanted to take out money above the premium you put in, you pay the surrender charge and an income tax.

In our system you take a loan against the cash value, not from the cash value. The cash value of the policy is actually your collateral.

You pay no interest during your lifetime and you don't need to pay it back. Interest and principal is taken from the death benefit, so your heirs do get less. Or you could pay back the loan if you prefer. Our system usually does not include paying it back.

But it does include keeping track to be sure that the policy stays in force. We watch to be sure that you are earning more or less what is projected, as we need to have the premiums paid from earnings. If the earnings are bit low one year, you may have to curtail some of your borrowing.

When you create your system using an IULI. and borrowing, you will be asked to choose between a fixed rate and a variable rate. The fixed is safer and completely predictable. You pay a % in interest, and the amount borrowed also earns some interest. It might even be a wash. In fact, if you own the policy for 10 years before you take the loan there may be 0% interest.

With variable rates you have less control over the interest rate you are charged, but your money can earn more as it still bears interest linked to a stock index. You're credited interest on funds that you borrowed minus a debit or interest charge for the loan.

As a practical matter, if you were retired and withdrew $20,000 for home improvement or the trip of a lifetime from your IRA, even with no penalty because you are over 59 1/2, you would have to pay taxes on that $20,000. By contrast, if you had a nest egg in the kind of solution system that we're talking about, you might borrow that $20,000 from yourself. You would not have to pay any taxes because it is borrowing, even though you are borrowing from yourself.

It does, however, have some impact on the death benefit in that policy. Nevertheless, if you're willing to accept that as opposed to paying taxes on $20,000, you have a tax-free income nest egg that you could draw upon over and over again depending on your needs.

Here is a comparative example of how this works. Assuming that the beginning amount is $600,000 in a traditional IRA and the needed withdrawal every year is $41,000, the following chart compares the result (at various age intervals) of keeping the funds in the traditional IRA and paying the taxes each year, moving the funds to a Roth IRA and paying the tax now, or moving the funds into the appropriate insurance vehicle, paying the tax now and taking tax-free policy loans.

Comparison: IRA, Roth IRA and An Alternative Tax Free Plan

Age	Year	IRA					RothIRA			An Alternative Tax Free Plan			
		IRA +/-	Tax (41.4%)	Net Spending	Growth (7.7%)	IRA Balance	Roth +/-	Growth (7.7%)	Roth Balance	Tax Free +/-	Accumulation	Surrender Value	Death Benefit
63	start					$600,000			$0				
64	1				$42,893	$642,893	$117,260	$7,836	$123,116	$200,000	$169,373	$55,732	$2,742,867
69	5	-$68,940	$24,930	$41,000	$47,420	$755,184	-$41,000	$25,924	$412,855	-$41,000	$573,721	$143,433	$354,808
72	9	-$68,940	$24,930	$41,000	$40,754	$648,019	-$41,000	$21,460	$341,752	-$41,000	$698,470	$124,076	$273,676
84	20	-$68,940	$24,930	$41,000	$6,396	$101,986	-$17,854	$0	$0	-$41,000	$1,730,000	$185,006	$271,310
86	22	-$34,873	$14,097	$19,978	$0	$0				-$41,000	$2,016,071	$251,666	$352,471
100	36									-$41,000	$5,954,347	$2,017,911	$2,017,911

As you can seen, the results are dramatic. The traditional IRA will run out of money at age 86. The Roth IRA will run out of money at age 84. The insurance policy will continue well past age 100 and will still maintain a $2 million dollar death benefit.

Chapter 5

The Pact With the Devil: Stock Market Volatility and Retirement

We cover: A perfect storm is brewing. I am concerned not only with stock market volatility or the next bear market, but also with bond market volatility. Interest rates are at a thirty year low by some standards, as interest rates creep up, fixed income or bonds are going to go backwards. There are solutions to escape excessive volatility by putting the correct system in place.

You will discover:

> ➤ The difference between a managed account and a separately managed account and why you need the latter

> ➤ The reasons for asset allocation and diversification and why they don't work to create the ideal retirement

> ➤ Solutions that protect you from devastating market volatility

What to do next:

> ➤ How about getting an illustration especially for you? Resister for a private consultation and illustration at www.fearfactorthebook.com

A gentleman came into my office for a consultation. He said, "Well, you know, I'm working with a broker, and he's got me in a managed account." I looked at his quarterly statement and found that his assets are typically in the same basket of mutual funds that we often see. His gains are diminished by a management fee or advisory fee tacked on in addition to all the mutual fund expenses.

What bothered me most was that he thought his holdings were handpicked for his goals. He had other portfolios that he understood were one-size-fits-all portfolios programmed to all buy the same thing at the same time. Still he thought it's better than struggling with decisions himself.

In fact, with the extra fees, he might be better off with a few low-cost mutual funds to which he pays periodic attention and no professional help at all.

By RONALD GELOK, with Adriane Berg

A Note From Adriane

There are many types of managed accounts to accomplish the ideal retirement. You want a **separately managed account,** not a programmed account.

One type of programmed account is often called a **wrap account** (a computer makes automatic changes in thousands of clients' portfolios all at the same time). Or there is a fund manager who dictates changes and they are made for everyone simultaneously. It's called a wrap because all the fees are wrapped up in one, including trading transaction fees and management fees.

If you are interested in understanding stock market movement, you can easily see how, if so many investors are doing the same thing, buying and selling the same way, the market moves big all at once. In fact, just before the Gulf War the market tanked for a few days. The issue was "programmed trading." These cookie cutter so-called managed accounts that you think are for you alone, all did the same thing at the same time.

Here's a key difference between these wrap account, mutual fund programs, and separately managed accounts. If you're in a mutual fund, the mutual fund manager has to adhere to the terms of the fund perspective. Let's say the fund prospectus describes the fund as a balanced fund and the fund must adhere to 60% equities and 40% fixed income. If we're in a rapidly declining market, that balance or that allocation still has to be maintained, so we can watch that mutual fund plummet in value.

Now, let's say we're in a separately managed account where the manager has broader discretion. If the manager feels conditions are like October 2008 and it makes sense to bring the majority of the portfolio back to cash for a time, the manager has the ability to do that.

Now obviously we're not guaranteeing that people in separately managed accounts never lose money, but we are saying we can be more in tune with what our clients are telling us, what's important to them about less volatility and less risk.

By RONALD GELOK, with Adriane Berg

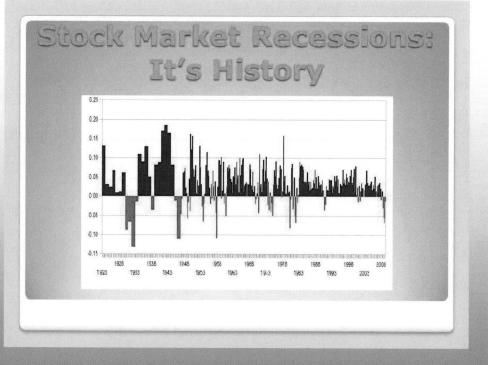

In fact, separately managed accounts are sometimes known as institutional money management for individuals. The investor gets an investment account and can give us direction or guidance on their goals, and we can provide money managers that meet those goals, then review and make changes at will.

By choosing the correct money manager or the correct portfolio manager and making sensible changes on an individual client basis, we have a better chance to limit our downside exposure.

Notice I said I had a better chance of protecting your downside. I can't guarantee that. No legitimate wealth advisor or money manager can or will give you a guarantee.

Yet I continue to offer money management because it makes sense for those people who say, "I like the idea of being empowered with safety and with guarantees, and I'm intrigued by the new and innovative offerings that some of the insurance companies are providing us, but clearly I can't put all of my funds in offerings from insurance companies."

By RONALD GELOK, with Adriane Berg

What I am leading up to is a two-part system. Part one, we have discussed in prior chapters, is a guaranteed insurance-based system to cover your income gap. Part two is a separately managed account to give you even more upside.

Asset Allocation, Diversification, and Hats Off to Harry

You've probably heard about asset allocation and diversification. Hopefully you have a mix of assets so that if one goes down, the other is up.

You may have read why you should diversify and allocate assets into different groups for better performance. The fancy term for this is modern portfolio theory. It emphasizes individual asset classes instead of individual stocks of particular companies.

Still, I think it's important for you to have a current overview since most of the concepts of what we technically call modern portfolio theory are not so modern.

Times have changed, yet thinking about asset allocation has remained pretty stagnant.

Let me explain.

Mutual funds that allowed people to invest in large numbers of stock companies simultaneously were really not available to the average Joe until the 1950s and even 1960s. Some of the first mutual funds were introduced in the 1930s, but you had to be fairly wealthy and have a broker to even know about them.

Of course, there was a sea change with mutual funds being introduced to all of us. Today, most preretirees are offered mutual funds and ETFs, or "exchange traded funds," in qualified plans by financial planners, on the Internet, and through e-trading services and even banks.

With the popularity of the mutual fund came the realization that mutual fund managers are selecting the stocks held within the fund and can make changes that affect your portfolio without you making any decisions whatsoever.

The question is, does this really make money?

By RONALD GELOK, with Adriane Berg

Many still believe that simply investing in an index like the S&P 500 or the Dow Jones Industrial Average or an index of small-cap stocks, or commodities that simply track how selected companies are doing, is just as good as having an active money manager.

Who is right?

No one is right or wrong. If you are not the type to pay attention to your money, you MUST have an advisor. When Malcolm Forbes was asked how he got so rich, he answered, "I pay attention."

A Note From Adriane

Harry Markowitz, the Father of Modern Portfolio Theory

Harry won the Nobel Prize in Economics for his idea about how best to invest. What he proved was that owning an individual stock or a group of stocks all in the same category of companies will not make you as much money as selecting a variety of asset classes and allocating your money among those classes. He suggested investing in a basket of stocks or a basket or mutual funds, which include large companies, small-cap, income production, commodities, value stocks, and international holdings.

By properly allocating, you do better than by picking one or two stocks, even winners, so long as you are holding your portfolio over time. That changed the character of brokers from then on. They went from stock pickers to asset allocation advisors.

With this technique came the concept of diversification. Within each asset class it might be wise to diversify. For example, if 25% of your portfolio is in large capitalized companies, perhaps you should diversify among many large capitalized companies.

That worked well with mutual funds that held the stocks of many such companies in which you could participate all at once. And so if you are careful in your selection, you have both asset allocation AND diversification.

By RONALD GELOK, with Adriane Berg

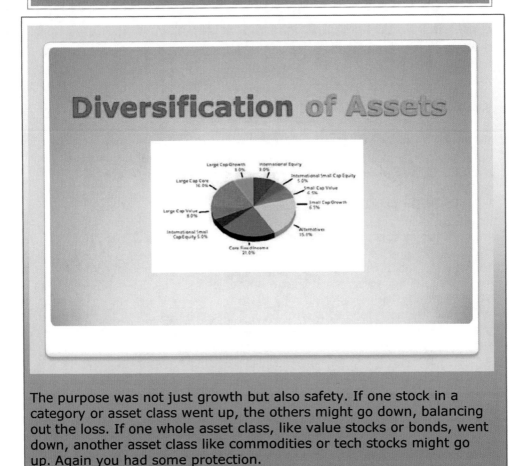

The purpose was not just growth but also safety. If one stock in a category or asset class went up, the others might go down, balancing out the loss. If one whole asset class, like value stocks or bonds, went down, another asset class like commodities or tech stocks might go up. Again you had some protection.

Modern portfolio theory worked pretty well until recently.

Times have changed and what was modern in the 1950s is not modern as we creep into the teens of a new century.

Because of computers, we have so much programmed trading that allocated portfolios tend to contain assets that all go up and down at the same time. Money managers are scrutinized, as they should be; they don't want to make mistakes and take chances. The result is that the money managers you rely on suffer from their own F.E.A.R. Factor.

Although it's the professional herd, they also tend to have a herd mentality. They do what their fellow fund managers do so that the assets you have so carefully diversified and allocated tend to move in lockstep. They're all affected by the same market pressures. And in

By RONALD GELOK, with Adriane Berg

many cases, the media has become so influential with both investors like you and financial professionals that a single statement on "exuberance" from the chairman of the Federal Reserve, a whisper that interest rates may change, political fears, or the national debt create in sync buys and sells worldwide.

In the old days, we looked to see whether a company was making money or not. Today, we look to see if it's in the right sector, if it is surrounded by a price bubble, if new technology will affect it, and if it trades with China. There are many more factors that affect selection. If we are wrong, there is a lot to lose.

In one sense, decision-making is more complex. In another sense, we have more information and investors are all making the same buy-and-sell decisions. It becomes difficult to place balance in a portfolio.

As I have said, I don't advise making asset allocation and diversification as your only means of protection from market volatility when you enter retirement. You simply cannot wait out the storm. You need a minimum income guarantee that you can count on. In the past we had pensions. Today we have Social Security and anything that we have saved that can yield a paycheck without working.

That is why I am constantly led to the solution of the indexed annuity, or IULI. In both cases, you are guaranteed that gains will not go backward and that you can structure a system that targets a definite amount of money you can receive each month or quarter.

Indexing: have your cake and eat it too

We are in rapidly changing times, and we need to identify solutions that fit the world we're in rather than the world the way we wish it was. We wish we were in a low-tax environment. We wish we were in a booming economy.

But we have to deal with reality; we like the concept of indexing: harnessing the upside of an index while protecting your principal against downside. This is where we're thinking outside the box and we're working with top-rated insurance companies who offer this type of system.

Now, it does have to be custom-designed to meet your individual needs and requirements. Then we have a program where we've got

By RONALD GELOK, with Adriane Berg

floors and guarantees in place, and still participate in a stock index. We're really accomplishing something here.

Now you try to create your system

Example of Indexed Account:
S&P500 Index with 100% Participation

Date	S&P500 Index Growth	Theoretical Interest Credited
1984	2.92%	2.92%
1985	26.23%	13%
1986	17.50%	13%
1987	-1.54%	0%
1988	12.88%	12.88%
1989	27.95%	13%
1990	-5.93%	0%
1991	15.87%	13%
1992	13.83%	13%
1993	6.41%	6.41%
1994	-1.73%	0%
1995	35.49%	13%
1996	20.89%	13%
1997	28.10%	13%
1998	23.52%	13%
1999	20.24%	13%
2000	-5.49%	0%
2001	-14.99%	0%
2002	-22.43%	0%
2003	23.18%	13%
2004	10.47%	10.47%
2005	5.63%	5.63%
2006	12.16%	12.16%
2007	2.43%	2.43%
2008	-39.37%	0%
2009	23.81%	13%
2010	13.39%	13%
2011	-2.18%	0%
2012	18.75%	13%
2013	25.35%	13%
Average	8.38%	8.11%

This table uses the historical performance of the S&P500 for the period 1984-2013. The chart illustrates how interest may be credited to an account. It assumes a growth cap rate of 13% and a participation rate of 100%

How about getting an illustration especially for you? Register for a private consultation and illustration at www.fearfactorthebook.com

Chapter 6

Would You Like to Build a Tax-Free Money Machine?

We cover: There is more than one way to create the tax-free money machine. You will have to choose between three types of systems to see which sits best with your philosophy. You may want some of each system.

We cover:

> ➤ Tax-free money machine systems

> ➤ The three systems

> ➤ How to choose

> ➤ Spend 15 minutes to create your future

> ➤ Annuity and insurance riders

What to do next:

> ➤ Visit www.RonaldGelok.com/F.E.A.R.Factor and check off the riders about which you are interested in learning more.

There are three ways to create your tax-free money machine using different systems. Let's take a look at each of them, from the most traditional to the most innovative.

1. The Roth IRA With a Distribution Plan

Senator Roth championed legislation that allows you to convert tax-deferred funds in an IRA or 401(k) into tax-free funds. You must pay the tax and roll over the funds to a Roth. Once you have a Roth, you can make after-tax contributions to it, not just convert already accumulated assets. After leaving the funds in for five years, any growth is completely tax-free. There are now Roth 401(k)s that many employers offer.

If you are younger, say a Millennial, you are probably better off using the tax-deferred plans as you have years of growth ahead of you. But five to ten years before retirement starting the Roth conversion process may be best. And if you are still making contributions, consider doing so in a Roth, even if you do not convert your current qualified funds to a Roth.

How a Roth works

When you are funding a Roth IRA, you do not get an upfront tax deduction as you do with the traditional IRA. This doesn't bother me. I prefer the Roth. If we were farmers and we had the option of paying taxes on the seed that we were buying at the start of the season or paying taxes on the sale of the ultimate harvest at the end of the season, which would we prefer?

It should be the first one, because seeds are worth less than harvests.

And yet we act to accomplish the second. To the extent that a person may be eligible to make Roth IRA contributions, they should do so.

The next step from there is to use a wealth manager and planner to work out a withdrawal program for you and to allocate your assets in a separately managed account.

This is great except for the following:

1. The government limits a person's ability to make Roth IRA contributions as their level of income goes up.

2. Many managers of separately managed accounts have a minimum, and you may not have enough assets to qualify for their minimums. So you are stuck with the wrap accounts or on your own.

3. Most important, you have no guarantees of performance.

I struggled with this question: Is there a system that could empower an individual to grow money free from current taxes like a Roth IRA with no limits on contributions? Is there a system that empowers a person to pull tax-free distributions, spendable money, out without incurring tax? Is there a system where the money could ultimately be passed income tax-free to family members at time of death?

2. How About a System Designed Around Indexed Life?

As you now know, there are certain tax code provisions that are extremely favorable toward insurance: specifically, the ability to grow cash value free from current tax and the ability to access the cash value free from taxation through a tax-free policy loan.

We aim to do that using indices for the growth of the cash value, and we want to do it in such a way that we minimize the mortality charges or cost of insurance.

The "secret sauce"

The secret sauce is that you can borrow and make money on the borrowed funds.

Here's how it works:

When you take a tax-free policy loan and use a variable loan rate of say 4.5%, if your indexed life policy earned 7.70% that year, you will have earned 7.70% on your policy's cash value, and your policy loan balance (money you took out and spent) will have earned 3.2%— unbelievable, but true.

For example, you have a policy with a cash value of $100,000. If you took a $30,000 loan out of your policy, you will earn $960 (7.70% – 4.5% = 3.2%) on the money you took out, in addition to the $7,700 earned (7.70%) on the cash value of your policy against which you did not borrow. (We even have companies that have caps on their variable loan rates.)

I call this the secret sauce. It allows you great flexibility in your life if you want to travel, give a gift, or regularly augment your cash flow.

The system allows for stock market type gains, without stock market type risk.

We need to insure that our nest egg will make as much money as it can. And that means including stock market participation in our retirement plan. Indexed Universal Life Insurance (IULI) uses your premium to partly pay for insurance that yields a death benefit and partly invests the rest to grow in accordance with certain stock market indices.

By RONALD GELOK, with Adriane Berg

True, you're not participating directly in the stock market as does an indexed mutual fund. That might have greater potential for gain but, at the same time, greater risk of loss.

Unlike indexed mutual funds, our system guarantees a floor or a protection from decline of principle. Asset protection, as we have reviewed in many prior chapters, is a very important feature for people who are pre- or just postretirement.

Indexing involves a contract with an insurance company that guarantees against loss but also caps the degree of gain to a specified percentage.

Let's assume an Indexed Universal Life Insurance contract offers 100% of what the S&P 500 does up to a cap of 13% or 14%. If the S&P goes up 15%, 18%, and our cap is 14%, well, we made 14%. On the other hand, if it's a year like 2008 and the S&P drops 39%, we did not lose a penny, and we still have the prior year's index linked interest credit available to us. It didn't go away.

I think that the greatest F.E.A.R. Factor, False Evidence Affecting Retirement, is that we're out of control, and this gives us some control.

Yes, there may be the price to pay in that we don't have the full upside potential in very bullish periods, but most people pre- and postretirement would be willing to take their 13% or 14% cap knowing that their loss could not be as devastating as it was in the year 2000 or 2008.

There's a better way to go than assuming massive risks of loss by trying to pick the mutual fund that did the best over the last 12 or 36 months.

What if you buy a policy and you don't like the way the system is working? After all you put in a big premium. Are you stuck? No. There is a rider that protects you, the Return of Premium Rider.

In no event will you receive back less than your premiums minus any partial withdrawals, if you surrender the policy. Still, my philosophy is never say yes to something just because you think you can get out of it.

By RONALD GELOK, with Adriane Berg

3. Don't Need Any Death Benefit? How About Indexed Annuities?

For those who do not need a death benefit or who are making contributions instead of one big lump-sum influx of cash, a third system is the indexed fixed annuity with a guaranteed lifetime benefit rider. We discussed this too in past chapters.

To review, this also requires a contract with an insurance company that guarantees income linked to a stock index. Once again, you do not have exposure in the event the index goes down, and there is a cap on your gain. Unlike the life insurance system, you will pay a tax when you withdraw from the annuity. Unlike the qualified plans, you are never forced to contribute or to withdraw.

When you want to withdraw, you are guaranteed a stream of income from your annuity at the rate the rider provided when you first signed the contract.

Here's an important heads-up.

In my opinion these are not for people about to retire because withdrawals within 5 to 10 years after the account opening may incur a surrender charge. So these annuities, with their benefits have a liquidity problem. Beware. On the good side, some contracts give all your money back if you want to reverse your decision within the first two years after signing the contract. But remember, never say yes to something just because you think you can get out of it.

So, I use these gingerly when I want to get guarantees, link to the stock market, and take money out in years to come to fill the income gap. You see, you can calculate exactly how much to commit to such annuities if you know how much the gap is, and then give yourself peace of mind that you will have an automatic withdrawal, not a do-it-as-you-go-along, hope-for-the-best system.

Funding Healthcare Expenses: Can You Afford to Live to 125?

My system has a feature to help the big problem that many of us are totally unprepared to face, long-term care and its costs.

The average couple, even with Medicare, will spend $225,000 during their lifetime out of pocket for healthcare because there's a lot that isn't covered by Medicare.

By RONALD GELOK, with Adriane Berg

As for Medicaid, it's essentially a welfare program; the likelihood of getting aid is small unless careful and aggressive moves are made. Even then, the eligible person's family may eventually suffer if the government steps up its collection procedure after the death of the Medicaid recipient and forecloses the home or other assets that were salvaged.

I want to approach healthcare in a broader context then just costs; that of restoring control over your retirement. I believe what people are looking for as they plan for retirement, or if they're already in retirement, is a sense of control. Too many people today feel that they're not in control.

To the extent that we use systems that give the ability to control loss, limit taxes, and protect against the extraordinary expenses of catastrophic illness, then we're empowering our future.

Both my parents were in good health when they entered their 70s. My father was taking a blood pressure pill and a cholesterol pill. My mother was taking a thyroid pill and something for osteoporosis, but neither one of them made it out of their 70s.

My father, at 77, had a massive stroke. It wasn't a stroke that sends somebody to a nursing home for the rest of their life. It was a stroke that ended his life. My mother was now six years into an Alzheimer's diagnosis, and my dad had been her primary caregiver. So, had we not done proper planning ahead of time, the financial losses would have amounted to everything they had worked a lifetime to accumulate.

Part of a system for an ideal retirement is that it protect assets for the benefit of yourself, your spouse, and ultimately for the benefit of children and grandchildren.

A Note From Adriane

Does any elder you know need help?

I recently was reminded of how much information we need as we get older. I was doing some sales training for a group in Maryland as they called prospects to invite them to a seminar. One of the gentlemen explained that he was 86 years old and that his wife had just been diagnosed at age 81 with Alzheimer's. He certainly could not attend

By RONALD GELOK, with Adriane Berg

any conference and lamented that he might himself die in the house. He was under such strain that he shared this with a cold-calling stranger. The young man politely said he understood and hung up.

I could not let it go. I called the gentleman again and explained that I was not calling about the conference but to offer help that he might need. He took notes for 20 minutes. I realized how fragile we are as we age. As a nuclear family, whether blended, extended, or modern, we are still insular.

As we age, we need knowledgeable people to help us. It's tough getting out of our self-sufficient shell and asking. I suggested he make a phone call to his County Department for the Aging to help him navigate available senior services and also visit www.N4a.gov, the federal government's system that divides our country into 633 parts, each with a separate information bank of support for elders and caregivers.

I also sent him to www.benefitscheckup.org and www.benefitsRX.org , both from The National Council on Aging. On those sites he can discover little-known entitlements from dentistry to prescriptions that could help.

Nothing is as important as family and friends. Sometimes that means having them pay for or contribute to at-home help. Perhaps one of the most important aspects of the Gelok approach is the use of video calling through Skype and other technologies. This means that family members or other loved ones from anywhere in the world can be part of a coordinated consultation.

Older adults tend to leave themselves in the shadows. Naturally, none of us want to relinquish autonomy or admit to frailty. In hiding the truth we often diminish our chances of living independently. A wise person acknowledges what is lacking and applauds with gratitude their strengths.

For an overview of the importance of communication and resources for elders, check out my ebook at http://www.adrianeberg.us/justkeeptalkingreg

By RONALD GELOK, with Adriane Berg

Are long-term care policies worth the price?

Most people are concerned about the expense of continuing to pay premiums year after year as they get older. I'm not saying that there's anything inherently wrong with traditional long-term care insurance, provided that you get into it at a young enough age.

For example, a lot of people don't know that there's such a thing as a single premium long-term care life policy. Let's suppose you've got $50,000 or $100,000 sitting in a money market account down at the local bank, and it's there because you want to keep that money liquid. Maybe it's there for a rainy day.

What rainy day could befall a person later in life? How about a change in health status? The idea here is you could take that same $100,000 or $50,000, deposit it with an insurance company, and buy a long-term care plus death benefit policy.

For example, if you're 65 years old and make a one-time $100,000 premium payment into a long-term care plus life policy, there's $120,000 to $140,000 income tax-free death benefit to your spouse or to your kids.

If you need long-term care, there might be $400,000 available to pay for home healthcare, assisted living, or long-term care. What's the real cost of that type of plan? Well, it's the lost interest that you didn't make on the money market account.

But the rates on traditional long-term care insurance are not guaranteed. In fact, the actuaries have underestimated what the utilization of long-term care services would be. People, because of advances in medical technology, are living long lifespans. And, as a result, they're coping with increased frailty and disability over a longer period of time. One can live upwards of 20 years with Alzheimer's.

So we've got to think outside the box. Why? We've seen major insurers in the last couple of years raise rates 40%, 50%, even more on in-force policyholders.

Insurance riders may come to the rescue.

An alternative to a single premium long-term care policy is an indexed life retirement account with what's known as a lifetime income benefit rider. This is a similar rider to what we discussed with annuities. For purposes of meeting future income needs, the account is guaranteed to compound at 6% or 6.5% per year. Then there's a specific level of income guaranteed for life.

To such a contract we can add a long-term care benefit to increase income in case of need. Let's say you're guaranteed 6% income for life at age 80. Then your health fails and you need home healthcare, assisted living, or nursing home care. Now your income could double, say, to 12%.

For example, you've got $40,000 a year of guaranteed lifetime income at retirement. If you need long-term care, that doubles to $80,000 per year for 5 years. That's one thinking-outside-the-box solution.

There are other riders that offer extra help in the face of long-term care needs. One is a chronic illness accelerated benefit rider. This works if you have an insurance-based system. If you have a death benefit as part of your system, up to 96% of the death benefit can be accelerated to pay for home healthcare, assisted living, or even nursing home expenses.

People tell me all the time, "Ron, I didn't even know that existed." That's the point I like to make: "We don't know what we don't know."

Riders, features, and contracts that lead to an ideal retirement in 15 minutes

We believe in taking a holistic approach to retirement planning, which means we want to help the whole person. When we sit down with somebody, we want to know what's really important to them about their future. What do you want to do with the balance of your lifetime? How do you want to spend your time? Then we want to put together plans to help you accomplish your lifestyle objectives.

By RONALD GELOK, with Adriane Berg

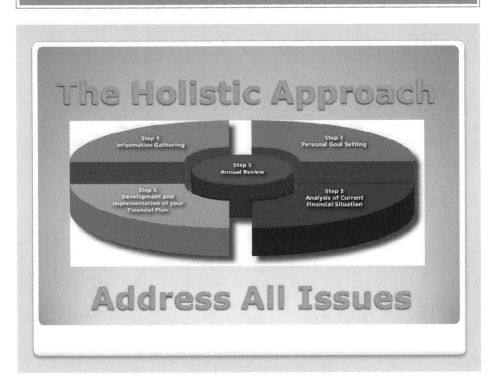

If you are thinking, "I really see myself being able to spend the winter in a warmer climate, but at the same time I want to be close to my grandchildren the majority of the year, and I don't want to worry about my monthly expenses or bills being met down the road, and I'm concerned about state estate taxes," only a system will address all these issues, including catastrophic illnesses or whatever soft spot a person may need to have addressed.

Revisit the list of riders at www.fearfactorthebook.com and check off the riders about which you are interested in learning more.

Chapter 7

Why do *YOU* F.E.A.R. to Think Outside the Box and Instead Follow the Herd?

We cover: The stories of the four people you meet in retirement, using them as iconic models of how the system works in real life. Why you need to think outside the box and not follow the herd.

You will discover:

- ➢ Why you go along with the herd

- ➢ Take a look around. The herd is not doing very well.

- ➢ Most people think inside the box. They saved in 401(k)s if they were disciplined. And even then they paid taxes. They also suffered recession after recession.

- ➢ By following the herd over and over again we act through fear and act too late.

- ➢ Each and every time that we follow the herd we do damage to our financial success.

- ➢ Our systems using indexed products do not follow the herd. You might call them contrarian and if you do act in a contrarian manner you should be proud of conquering the F.E.A.R.

What to do next:

- ➢ Please visit www.fearfactorthebook.com for real-life examples of people who perhaps could be your new reference point, your new herd. These are the stories of people who did not get scared by a word but got engaged in really thinking about the purpose of what they're doing.

We all know the problem. We buy high. We sell low. This happens because we wait for confirmation from others, particularly when it comes to the stock market. Most people are planning to work in retirement, some because they want to but most because they have to. It's no joke to think about the elderly serving fries at McDonald's or greeting you at Wal-Mart. We are grateful that these major corporations hire older adults, but sad that older adults need to do this

By RONALD GELOK, with Adriane Berg

work. Most baby boomers in their 60s are struggling not to have to take Social Security early, just because they won't have the retirement income to wait out until age 70 when they get Social Security maximum benefits.

Why do we follow the herd so frequently?

One reason is habit; another is that the media covers only certain financial stories and offers only certain financial solutions.

For example, financial TV shows are devoted to the stock market. There may be *Wall Street Week*, but you will never see *Insurance and Annuity Week* on the air.

How do some of the things that are written by journalists, writers, or even bloggers make us follow a herd that isn't really doing very well?

It's human nature to want to be validated. When the media touts an investment strategy, we pay attention. We feel safer when our perception is that everybody is doing it, so it must be the right thing to do.

Just earlier today somebody cancelled an appointment because they read something that presented false evidence that definitely affected their retirement.

One of the advisors in our office had recommended that this person consider rolling over a portion of his retirement account to a fixed annuity that offered index-linked interest, lifetime income guarantees, an income doubler feature for long-term care expenses, and strong liquidity features.

Now here's the sad part.

This particular individual had a $200,000 IRA in CDs earning next to no interest, and $300,000 in a very aggressive brokerage account. So, on the one hand he has substantial loss exposure on his IRA as far as the brokerage element. Then, on the other hand, he's earning next to nothing on another portion of his IRA.

Now, he went on the Internet. He found a couple of articles that were inaccurate, ill-informed, and ill-written and were critical of indexed annuities. (I'm not saying that all index annuities are ideal. There are some that are way better than others, and we help clients differentiate between the better ones, in our view, and the ones we don't like.)

He became tainted by misinformation. Because he saw it on a website, he thought it must be credible. Sadly, he said, "Well, I think I'm just going to leave everything as is." Sometimes leaving everything as-is becomes a prescription for disaster.

If you're going to continue to think the same way you always have, you're going to continue to get the same thing you've always gotten. It isn't easy, and we respect the fact that it's hard to make a change.

A Note From Adriane

How to Use this Book Revisited

At this stage, it's important for you to understand how very free you are to get help and support with no obligation. I want to give you a personal insight on how I think it would serve you best to use the materials that we have provided here.

In the introduction you were encouraged to contact Ronald Gelok & Associates right away and make an appointment. By now you should have done that. You can do a lot of groundwork before the meeting. Start by doing the exercises on the interactive website. Then speak with your significant other and have them do the same or give them a report of where you have blind spots, income gaps, tax exposure, and the other issues you're going to discover for yourself in this book. Listen together to one or two of the webinars that you will find in the Education Center at www.RonaldGelok.com. If you are in any way able, I would attend a live seminar of Ron's.

Then KEEP that appointment.

Don't hesitate in getting help because you think you do not have enough money or enough time, or because you already have a plan you think is fixed in stone. You owe it to yourself to have all the tools you need to plan your future.

Are you destined to follow the herd?

Many baby boomers, people born between 1946 and 1964, who are now on the doorstep of retirement, started investing in the 1980s and 1990s. They experienced tremendous growth during that period of time. Then they got really slapped backwards in the 2001 and 2002 crashes. Since they were still pumping money into their 401(k), they didn't feel the loss of net worth as much as if they were already in retirement.

Then they lost money horrendously in 2008. But, by 2012, 2013, or so, they had made it back and have been profitable since then.

Ask yourself, what would it be really like if we went through another 2008? This million-dollar 401(k) that you're counting on to fund your income for the next 30 years turns into a $620,000 401(k). What would that feel like, and should we do anything before the next bear market occurs to protect some of that money?

Set up a system for protection. But there is one caveat: If you can't understand it, don't do it.

I think we need to talk about financial systems and products for what they do, not necessarily what they're called or what their labeled.

Here is a real conversation I had recently:

By RONALD GELOK, with Adriane Berg

Client: "Well, Ron, I've got my 401(k) here. I just retired. I need to figure out what's appropriate for a rollover for me. And I'm concerned on the one hand about stock market risk. In the next bear market, I could lose hundreds of thousands of dollars, and I don't want to be positioned where that could happen.

"I'm also concerned with interest rates being so low and having no place to go but up. I don't want to lose money on my long-term bond values as interest rates go up.

"Is there anything out there that I could own to position a portion of that 401(k) rollover so that I don't have to worry about my account going backward when the interest rates rise, or when the stock market plummets in the next bear market cycle? And I have the potential to make a reasonable rate of return and know that my income requirements can be met?"

Me: "Well, what if we had an IRA account that did all of those things? Would that be a good fit for you?"

Client: "Yeah, that would be wonderful. Is there anything that does that?"

Me. "Absolutely. We can get that from an insurance company."

Client: "Oh. You mean an annuity. I don't want that."

(I'M IMMEDIATELY SHUT DOWN BY THE HERD MENTALITY.)

Me: "Well, if we called it a frazmataz and it did all these things, would you then want it?"

One of the things that we are doing at Ronald Gelok & Associates is creating a new herd.

Four People You'll Meet In Retirement

1. **Gertrude**: I had a review meeting with a client who was a recent widow. It was kind of a sad meeting because we were filling out death claim paperwork on a life insurance policy that her late husband had purchased.

By RONALD GELOK, with Adriane Berg

She didn't imagine, five years ago when they purchased the policy on his life, that he would only live another five years. Everybody was telling them, no, you're too old for life insurance. You shouldn't be buying life insurance in your 60s. That's a dumb thing to do.

That was herd advice, but terrible advice. She's now dealing with the reality of losing one of the Social Security checks. If one spouse passes away, the government no longer pays Social Security checks to both spouses anymore. And she's dealing with the reality of her husband's pension being cut by 50%. Had we not put that life insurance in place, she'd be forced to sell her house, move into an apartment, and make lifestyle choices that she shouldn't have to be making at age 70. That's one real-life example, not necessarily a happy one, but a real-life example.

2. **Eddie:** I had dinner recently with a client, and he brought a statement on an annuity account that he had opened with us. This was a fixed annuity account that offered index linked interest. Guess when he opened this account? In the spring of 2008. He said, "At the time I opened up this account with you, all my friends told me that I was an idiot, that I should never be putting money into an annuity with an insurance company. Why would I want to do that?"

Well, meanwhile, his friends lost hundreds of thousands of dollars. He's never lost a dime. His interest credit in the last 12 months was over 16%; linking his interest credit to the S&P 500 gave him the upside without the downside. Imagine how happy he was that he thought for himself.

3. **Susan:** I have another client who needed additional income in retirement but didn't want to pay through the nose in taxes. We properly structured an Indexed Universal Life Insurance contract to generate tax-free income through a policy loan. This generates spendable dollars that do not incur a penny of tax liability. Once again, we like to deal with people who think for themselves, who aren't afraid to do the right thing because it's contrary to a magazine article.

4. **Julius:** I met a fellow at one of my client appreciation events who said to me that he had been doing so beautifully he took it upon himself to tell his friend, a poker buddy, because that fellow was letting his money languish in what I call "certificates of disappointment."

By RONALD GELOK, with Adriane Berg

He was frustrated because the fellow did not come in for a consultation with us. He said to me, "I sure hope he's not letting his money just sit there." That was his exact phrase.

What struck me was that they're probably very good friends. They're probably around the same age. They probably have a similar background. They certainly like each other a lot. Yet they probably are leading two very different retirement lifestyles.

My client is very secure. He's very happy. He was making his 16%. But his friend is probably worried every day, unless he took action.

Now, visit www.fearfactorthebook.com and look at some real-life examples. You're going to read about people who perhaps could be your new reference point, your new herd. These are the stories of people who did not get scared by a word but got engaged in really thinking about the purpose of what they're doing.

Chapter 8

How Many Thousands Per Month Tax-Free Do You Want?

We cover: Worksheets to determine how much to convert from tax-free to tax-deferred based on how much income you want after retirement.

You will discover:

> ➢ A review of the points made in the first seven chapters.

What to do next:

> ➢ Now fill out the worksheets found at www.fearfactorthebook.com and see what's right for you.

Review of major points so far:

> ➢ **Too much tax deferral is dangerous to your wealth.** If you are a baby boomer or younger, you are aware that pension plans have disappeared. Unless you are a teacher, a police officer, a firefighter, or in certain nonprofit careers, what you have is a 401(k), 403B, or other tax-deferred retirement savings plan. In some respects they are all pacts with the devil. They are the result of pulling the rug out from under a retirement future and forcing us to save independently to create that future. As a come-on, in some people's opinion, and as an incentive in others' opinion, the IRS gave you tax deferral.

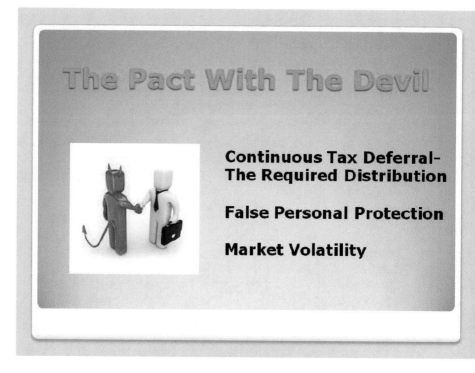

- Most people wait at least until age 65 to begin taking withdrawals, at which time those withdrawals are taxable as ordinary income.

- If you decide to wait to take withdrawals, you are forced to take them in the April 15th after you reach 70 ½.

- I know it's a strong statement, but I do think that too much tax deferral can be a pact with the devil. For example, we've all been told that we should sock away as much money as we possibly can in employer-sponsored plans like 401(k)s and 403(b)s and 457 plans because, when we retire we'll be in a much lower tax bracket. But that just is not the case for most people that we counsel.

- They find that they're in the same tax bracket they were when working or one bracket higher because they've lost deductions for mortgage interest and the dependent children exclusion. They may still have income coming in from Social Security, perhaps pension and/or rental income, as well as dividend income.

By RONALD GELOK, with Adriane Berg

➤ The income that is coming out of the qualified plans is all taxed at ordinary income tax rates. It can propel somebody into a higher tax bracket. It can trigger a higher rate of taxation on Social Security income. Too much tax deferral is not a good thing.

➤ In addition to socking money away tax-deferred, we also wait as long as possible to take the money out. We compound this pact with the devil by holding money in qualified plans as long as possible.

➤ If you had been talking to me 15 years ago, and you were in your early 60s, I might have said, "Let's continue to safely get as much growth as we can on the retirement accounts, and let's not take any money out until you're 70 1/2. That was the conventional wisdom then and, for a lot of advisors who are not up to speed today, it's still the conventional wisdom.

➤ But if we're looking at it from the perspective that tax rates are likely to be significantly higher in the future because of the way our government spends money, then it makes more sense to take some money out in our 60s rather than wait until 70 1/2.

➤ This is where we get into a whole area of planning that's overlooked and neglected called distribution planning. We must figure out what makes the most sense for an individual or a couple in the timing of withdrawals from their qualified plans or IRAs.

➤ The decumulation or distribution stage really is neglected.

➤ Your RMD is taxed at a higher rate than, say, long-term capital gains for most people. Depending on the state you live in, it's also subject to state income taxes.

The Required Minimum Distribution

Applies to:

Employer Sponsored Plans

Qualified Plans

401(k)'s

403(b)'s

457's

By April 1 of the year following you're the year in which you turn 70 1/2

You must take a distribution from your retirement in the amount of 3.65%

And the percentage increases through your 70's

> Most of your gains would probably have been taxed as capital gains, but because of deferral they are taxed as income.

> The stock market goes into recession approximately every 8 years and takes about 18 months to recover. This is not so bad when you have 10 to 30 years to invest. This is a disaster when you are about to retire or in retirement already. Add that to the taxation of what little is left, and you are in trouble because of your pact.

Now do the worksheets found at www.fearfactorthebook.com, and see what's right for you.

Chapter 9

Can We Really Stack the Deck in Our Favor?

We cover: Here's how you stack the deck.
- You get tax-free income
- You get a floor under which your assets can never fall
- You retain the power to take an advance on the death benefit insurance portion of your system should you need long-term care
- You leave a legacy
- You have a guarantee against market volatility
- You get market gains participation
- The cards are stacked in your favor, but it takes nerve. It takes nerve to pay taxes early, which has always been contrary to the conventional wisdom. It takes nerve to invest in the stock market through a system rather than through individual mutual funds and ETFs. It takes nerve to look at your financial future and face the potential shortfall and then actually do something about it

You will discover:

- Proof that controlling loss and minimizing taxes is the name of the game

- Numbers showing how one couple with herd mentality did against another couple who prepaid taxes and had a guarantee against loss

- Scenarios for single individuals

- Scenarios for early use of insurance benefits for long-term care.

What to do next:

- Visit our website, www.fearfactorthebook.com you will find streamlined, simple paperwork. If you'd really like to create your retirement future in 15 minutes, fill out those worksheets and get them to us. You'll see instructions on how to do that. Have an in-office or virtual conference with Ronald Gelok & Associates and then start on that guidance where trust is built, questions are answered.

By RONALD GELOK, with Adriane Berg

I can and will show you how to stack the deck in your favor and how others have done so. But I can't help you if you are constitutionally bound to money market funds, mutual funds, or individual stocks and bonds alone. I am a money manager. I use all these vehicles for clients. And they do well. But only a system can stack the deck for you. And only if you refuse to follow the herd, at least with some of your money can you create a system.

Sometimes following the herd can lead right over the side of a cliff.

It's interesting. Just before I started to write this chapter, we did one of our client appreciation dinners. As you know by now, we don't advertise. We educate. That's how we attract new clients and keep current ones.

A client came up to me at the event, gave me a big bear hug, and with tears in his eyes (I'm not exaggerating) said, "You know, Ron? I've got to tell you, meeting you was an answer to prayer." Quite frankly, I was humbled, and I was overwhelmed by him telling me this.

Why the gratitude? What our team did for this client years ago was to set up a tax-free income plan. We called upon our expertise in dealing with little-known provisions in the tax code, and we structured an unbelievable program using Indexed Universal Life Insurance to generate a tax-free income for him.

He's borrowing out his own money tax-free. At the same time, he's earning money on anything that he hasn't borrowed with a guaranteed floor; yet if the market indices we chose go up he will participate, up to a 17% gain. Sure, if the market makes over 17% he doesn't get that, but that's the tradeoff to stack the deck in his favor. If the market is that good and he's making that much, the 17% cap is something we all wish we could actually achieve.

Here is another great "stack the deck" strategy.

My client also makes money on the money he borrows. Stay with me here. This is the second time I am giving an explanation to you and I want you to get it straight. Remember the rule, "Never invest in anything you don't understand."

I don't think a system that has you borrow your own money for tax-free income and keeps the borrowed funds on the books to still earn market index growth is too complicated to understand. When we first heard about the concept of a mutual fund, it sounded complicated to us. When we first hear about the mortgage concept of flexible-rate loans, variable-rate loans, and fixed-rate loans, it seemed like a jumble at first. But, if you're working with advisors who know this area, who are willing to take the time with you to educate you and bring you up to speed on it, a lot can be accomplished.

So how did the client keep making money on his borrowed funds?

There are insurance contracts that give you a choice of borrowing at a fixed and certain rate or at a variable rate. In some years the fixed rate is best because interest rates are low but might rise. If I choose the certainty of the fixed rate, the borrowed money usually does not earn anything.

If I choose a variable rate, I will likely pay more interest, but the amount borrowed still earns money. For example, a fixed rate loan might cost 1% interest for the first 10 years and 0.10% interest thereafter. You might use that in certain years when you think rates will stay low.

In the same year a variable rate loan may cost 4%. If you took $30,000 as a tax-free policy loan, there's interest of 4%, but that same $30,000, if it earned index-linked interest of 8%, would have a positive 4% credit. It's an absolute mindblower. People say, "Well, wait a minute. Tell me that again."

By RONALD GELOK, with Adriane Berg

That's almost like walking into the bank and saying to the banker, "Listen, I'd like to take a loan, and I'd like you to pay me interest on the amount of the loan that I'm walking out with."

When you make an arrangement to borrow out a certain amount of money, you're not stuck forever borrowing every year. Let's say the next year you win the lottery. You don't need that much money. You can make changes as to how much you're going to borrow out.

You have tremendous flexibility. If one year you need more money, you can take more. The next year, if you need less, you take less. You're not locking yourself into a particular rate or income distribution. People like that flexibility.

Yet few people seem to know about this strategy. It's so interesting to me when I explain this concept at my seminars and people turn to each other and say, "What did he just say?" You know what it is? This vocabulary, this terminology is not familiar to all of us.

So what's the catch?

Well, actually, this works very well in low-interest-rate environments like we're in now, where the stock market and the indices that are linked to them are doing very well. There's a net gain by borrowing. It's not so unusual. It's just that people don't think that way.

In Europe, many people borrow money in one country because interest rates on borrowing are low, and they deposit their borrowing in another country that offers higher interest rates. It happens all the time. It's called an "interest rate sandwich." This is what we mean by stacking the deck in our favor by thinking out of the box. Sometimes that same interest rate sandwich is referred to by a little fancier term as a "favorable arbitrage." Does that sound smarter?

As you can see, this borrow-and-keep earning concept stacks the deck beautifully in a low-interest-rate environment. So, it's fair to ask me, "Ron, what if I put this plan in place and things change. Say in 10 or 15 years, we're in a high interest rate environment?"

I answer, "Well, what if we could bring a system or a product forth that had a cap on the loan rate? Would that then make sense for you?"

You'd most likely respond, "Well, yes, of course. Is there such a thing?"

By RONALD GELOK, with Adriane Berg

Yes, indeed. You can opt for variable rate borrowing with a cap on that interest rate.

It gives me a thrill to see the relief and smile on faces when people make a discovery.

To me it is a discovery when you find out something new that really makes a difference to your financial future and you are in control. Knowledge has just gotten so specialized in our society today, and what we bring to the table is what I would call the right know-how for today's times.

Ronald Gelok & Associates logo and slogan is "Trust and Know-How." This is clearly the know-how part. We'll get to the trust part in a moment. When we talk about stacking the deck in our favor, we're really not talking about pie in the sky or things that are too good to be true or taking risks. What we're talking about is basic, solid knowledge from somebody who can guide you through.

Now, let's take the trust part of our slogan; how do you gain trust and guide people through making a major life decision? I feel trust is something that's earned over time. We invest an extraordinary amount of time. For example, the very first interaction that a client has with us is a diagnostic interaction, like when you go to the doctor's office but not as scary.

The doctor can't guess how to solve or deal with your ailment if you don't share what your condition is. In our first interaction with somebody, we're going to ask them a lot of questions, totally confidential of course, about what is important to them, what their situation is, and what level of assets they have to work with.

Then, in our second interaction, we're going to present our ideas. Not for purposes of them plunging into anything, but to get an understanding of what might be a really better way to go.

Then, in our third interaction, we're going to have a question-and-answer session/implementation meeting. When all questions are answered to the client's satisfaction, then and only then are we moving forward. So we have a process that's tried and true that we take prospective clients through, and it's very relaxing. It's very reassuring.

By RONALD GELOK, with Adriane Berg

I can't guarantee that we can help everybody who goes through that process. But, if you do, I can guarantee you will come away a lot better informed about your situation and your options.

Now, I am excited about this book as it cuts your planning time to just a few minutes and gives you access to us in seconds. And we take the time to help you. If you wish, you are welcome to visit us personally in our office, as well.

If it's really not convenient to get to our main office in Parsippany, New Jersey, we cover all consultations completely via Skype, via the Internet, and paperwork via Federal Express. That's the beauty of today's technology.

Now, let's get back to stacking the cards in our favor.

Just to recap, the whole idea is to be in a position of control. What is it that we want to control? We want to be able to control loss or limit loss, and we want to be able to control or limit taxes.

Now, you might say, well, we can't limit taxes. We're not the legislators writing the tax laws. But if we use financial vehicles that have favorable tax code provisions associated with them, then in effect that's exactly what we're doing.

One properly structured system for tax-free income requires that we utilize IULI, and we custom design it in such a way as to limit the mortality charges or costs of insurance by limiting the death benefit to the amount that's appropriate.

We custom design this to allow enough time for the cash value to grow using index-linked interest with reasonable caps on the upside, say 13%, 14%, or 17%, depending on the program. We keep what we make in good years. We avoid losing any of the index-linked interest gains to our cash value in the bad years. And we're able to comfortably draw tax-free policy loans, which create real spendable dollars for us to supplement our other income in retirement.

It's a win/win, and it's refreshing to see that there is a way to feel secure about our retirement future because we're not getting the best news from the media right now, particularly for us baby boomers.

Time for a special invitation

Visit our website, www.fearfactorthebook.com and you'll find very streamlined, simple paperwork. If you'd really like to create your retirement future in 15 minutes, fill out those sheets and get them to us. You'll see instructions on how to do that. Have an in-office or virtual conference with Ronald Gelok & Associates, and then start on that guidance where trust is built, questions are answered.

Chapter 10

Is There Really a Way to Keep What's Earned in the Good Years and Not Lose in Bad Years?

We cover: What is the guarantee for earnings, what is the guarantee of no loss, what is the guarantee of tax-free borrowing, what is the guarantee of early use of insurance proceeds?

You will discover:

> ➤ The criticism of the system—what is fair criticism and what is not
> ➤ Criticisms include high commissions and fees, phony guarantees, and what to look for to protect yourself
> ➤ How the Gelok team protects you

What to do next:

> ➤ Review the easy worksheets: www.fearfactorthebook.com

I've pointed out the devastating effect of stock market volatility resulting in loss, particularly around retirement age or right after retirement, and as we get into our 80s and 90s. Now, that's really a terrible time for the stock market bubble to burst. I've done it earlier in the book, and several times, but I feel I should explain the effect of a recession on us once more.

The Mathematics of Stock Market Recovery

Decline Amount	Advance Required to Breakeven
25%	33%
33%	50%
50%	100%
75%	300%
90%	900%

By RONALD GELOK, with Adriane Berg

I am about to criticize my own recommended system and yet ask you to stick by it. So, I want us to have in mind how much there really is to lose if there's a pullback in the stock market, and how little it takes to protect against that. That will explain why, despite some flaws in the system, it may be better for you than stock market risk taking or low-income risk-averse investing.

The potential for loss of assets in the market is especially concerning right now because of where we are in the economic cycle and how high the market is. I'm reminded of a prospective client whom I met several years ago at a similar point in time where the market was nearing a peak. He came into the office, and his mindset was to find a financial advisor who would assure him of making 10% per year every year. I told him I couldn't make that guarantee.

I said, "You know what? We're not a good fit for one another because nobody can guarantee you that, and I'm not going to make a promise that I can't keep." And so we shook hand. We parted friends.

Low and behold, a couple years later, after the market dropped 39%, I actually ran into this gentleman in the Home Depot. He wasn't shopping at Home Depot. He was working there with that orange vest on.

Yep.

He sheepishly came over to me and asked me if I remembered him. I said, "Yes." His sad admission was, "You know, you were right. I should have gotten safer."

I have always blamed myself. I should have explained that he could use IULI to both participate in the market and get a guarantee against loss. You see, we were both so focused on guaranteeing or not guaranteeing gain that I failed to emphasize the more critical importance of guaranteeing against loss. I will never know if he would have taken heed, especially as he would have had to cap his gains. But maybe he could have been at Home Depot buying paint for his new man cave instead of working in the paint department.

By RONALD GELOK, with Adriane Berg

A Note From Adriane

Be a Phoenix

I'm sure you know about the mythical creature called the Phoenix. The Phoenix rises from the ashes after a crash and burn. Some of us must become a Phoenix. Whether 2008 took the toll, whether you've made some miserable mistakes in your past, it's time for a breakthrough. There are many motivational books and spiritual environments, which will help. But I have found one thing that turns lemons into lemonade instantly. It is this simple statement: "You are not your situation."

You desire to travel the world but surely can't afford it. Why do you love to travel? Can you inspire others to do so? Can you become a group leader for any of the major travel packagers that give you free travel if you can bring them 10 paying customers?

So you want to start your own business and have never succeeded in the past. Have you visited www.SCORE.org and gotten the advice of veteran successful business people free of charge? Have you taken a course at your local lifelong learning institute that retools you for your future?

What is the magic potion that will lift you to your next stage in life? It is your own energy and willingness to make a change.

This has everything to do with the income gap. No financial planner is a magician. Yes, we have encouraged you from the beginning of this book to dream big. Once you have maximized your guaranteed and probable income and still there is a gap, you must fill it with creativity.

Notice that I did not say you have to abandon your dream. You just have to find another way to accomplish it. Once you have identified that need and you know your target, there are hundreds of ways to reach your goal creatively. This is particularly true in the world of today's Boomer. There is so much help and advice out there. There are armies of groups online that share travel expenses; there are house-swapping opportunities; there are countywide programs for younger people to live with you and subsidize your housing costs or your caregiving needs; there are freelancers who will support the tasks you need to start a business. There is a Purpose Prize for boomers that have achieved life goals that benefit others. Free yourself to find creative angles.

By RONALD GELOK, with Adriane Berg

> I really don't believe in think and grow rich. But I do believe that if you think wrong you cannot approach or even achieve fundamental goals. That's why the Phoenix is such a powerful symbol of hope. From dust came greatness.

You see, one of the things it's very easy for us to forget in bull markets and in rah-rah times is what can happen in a pullback.

We experience a recession at least every eight years, but how long does it take to recover, and why is it so tough when it's right before or right after retirement?

When we're still actively at work and experience a bear market, we don't fully realize the impact of a recession even when it arrives. Our paycheck is coming in. If we are saving for retirement, we have new money coming out of each paycheck funding the 401(k). If the market is low that just means we are buying low. It averages out over time; so there's dollar cost averaging working for us (putting the same amount of money into the same investment every week, month, or other period so that the purchase price averages out over time.)

But once we're retired and there's no paycheck coming in, the effect of a bear market can be devastating. The S&P 500 index, which is a broad representation of the overall market, dropped almost 39% in 2008. That's almost a 40% decline. Now if there's a 40% decline, you need a 67% increase just to get your money back to where it was.

Now let's suppose at the same time you're retired and you're taking 5% or 6% of your net worth out that year for income. In effect, you are down 45% instead of 40% because of the income withdrawal. Now you need an 82% increase just to get your principal back to where it was. Most people will say, "If that happened to me, I don't know what I would do. I don't want to have to go back to work." Yet, people are being blind about the potential for loss.

Let's be honest with each other. We can be quite slavish to the herd mentality because there is a feeling of greed and euphoria when we see a market going up. That's why I want to keep that statistic in front of you: You need to make 67% to make up for a 40% loss. I think we all have a gut feeling that we would like to protect against loss, but we really don't realize how devastating it can be and how

By RONALD GELOK, with Adriane Berg

hard to recover. Of course, we don't have the time to make up for it, if we're right before or right after retirement.

The system I am describing gives the guarantees we need against loss and more.

The reason I think we're so skeptical is that we're always hearing that there are no guarantees, particularly with mutual funds or individual stocks or even with bond funds. By both state and SEC law, financial companies and financial professionals must be very careful **NOT** to make guarantees. How come, with an annuity or various insurance products, there can be this guarantee if the stock market goes down or your index goes down or whatever you're linked to goes down, there's a floor below which you cannot go?

How could there be a guarantee in one arena and not a guarantee in another arena?

We're really talking about two different arenas. I'll give you an example: A single woman who built her own business told me, "I'm looking for some help managing my money, and I want to explore what's out there in the universe of managed investment accounts. Do you have access to portfolios that are managed with capital preservation in mind and income generation as a goal, and are there any money managers out there that maybe didn't lose money in '02 or '08 that we could look at?"

I answered, "We do have access to such programs and managers, and I personally could look after your account." And then she said the magic words, "Are my returns guaranteed? Is this guaranteed not to lose money? Is this guaranteed to produce a particular rate of return?"

I had to say, "No." Past performance is no guarantee of future results when we're dealing with investments and securities. But when we're talking about contracts with insurance companies, these are not classified as securities. They are contracts between an individual and an insurance company where we can legitimately say that there are guarantees in place, while we can't use this word *guarantee* when we're talking about risk-based investments.

Maybe because I am an attorney by background, I am a little upset about the nomenclature used to describe the systems I like. These are contracts. Unfortunately, they're all called annuities or indexed life or some such language and all these terms apply to many different kinds of contracts. Some are good for you and some aren't. When we use these words that are emotionally charged, it's easy to make blanket statements that annuities aren't good, or they pay too little, or the commissions are too high. You know some of the criticisms are and some aren't true. Those that fit the system I like carry that magic guarantee of a floor.

Now let's get as specific as we can. What is the guarantee, really? And what price do you pay for that because we're all realistic. You pay a price for everything.

Let's use an example easy for everybody to understand and define all the jargon. I am going to give you a definition of each and every difficult concept.

I'm going to take this $100,000, and I'm going to deposit it with an insurance company into an *annuity contract*. It's a *fixed annuity* contract that offers *index-linked interest* and has a *rider* that offers *lifetime income guarantees.* What does all that vocabulary or terminology really mean?

Annuity: A financial product sold by financial institutions that is designed to accept and grow funds from an individual and then pay out a stream of payments to the individual at a later point in time.

All Annuities Are Not the Same

Immediate Annuities	Deferred Annuities
• Single Life Income	• Traditional Fixed Annuity
• Joint Life Income	• Fixed Indexed Annuity
• Period Certain	• Variable Annuity

Contract: A legally enforceable agreement; in our terms the contract is between you and the insurance company. That's why picking the right company is crucial. There are services like A. M. Best that grade companies for their reserve, fiscal responsibility, and much more.

Fixed annuity: We will get a fixed rate on our money. All fixed annuities have something in common. They don't go backward. They only go forward. But, if you buy in low-interest-rate times, you could be stuck with low interest and really suffer if inflation sets in.

Index-linked interest: When we talk about index-linked interest, we're able to link our rate of interest to the performance of an external market index like the S&P 500 or the Dow or the Nasdaq or some other index. Now here's where the catch comes in; you're not getting 100% of the gains if you're protected against 100% of the losses. There are caps on the earnings.

Rider: A part of the contract with the insurance company under which you get certain features. In return you pay for the benefits in the rider.

Lifetime: You may think you know what that means. But part of the contract defines whether a lifetime refers to your lifetime, or your spouse's or your joint lives, so long as you both live regardless of who passes away first.

Income: Income we refer to can either be a distribution that is taxable sent to you from earnings or a tax-free borrowing that you elect to take.

Guarantees: Let's say a contract capped your earnings at 2% per month; the most that you could ever earn is 24% per year. Let's say it was a year where the market went up consistently, and that gain was realized. That gain, once credited, is now part of the principal. So, if the following year is a repeat of 2008 and the index falls off a cliff and goes backward 39%, none of the prior gain that was credited the prior year is lost. It's still there. And that's the case year after year.

Most of the people that we serve are not looking to hit a home run every year. They're content with getting some of the gains and locking up those gains in good years, as long as they don't have to give back any of those gains in the bad years.

We said in prior chapters that you should be making a system and not a plan, and this is what we mean. When we make a plan, we can't

By RONALD GELOK, with Adriane Berg

keep to that plan if the stock market is not planning with us. Even if we could make all the right decisions on day one, if on day ten the stock market changes, our plan is out the window.

When we have a system, we have more than just a plan. We also have enough guarantees built in to know that we can carry out that plan. Now part of that plan for most of my clients is to have tax-free income all of their life.

Long-term care revisited

All of us have worked very hard for what we've accumulated and saved for retirement. And most of us also want to be able to leave a legacy to benefit our children and, in particular, our grandchildren. I'm reminded of that quote from the Book of Proverbs that a good man leaves an inheritance to his children's children.

Legacy Plus Long-Term Care Coverage

Recently, I was referred a client whose husband had passed away about a year and a half ago. She's got a $10 million estate, but she doesn't want to manage it. Her son and daughter are very active professionals. They don't have time to manage Mom's money. You might say with $10 million, she doesn't have to worry about long-term care. She could pay it herself.

Her mindset was different. She felt that her husband and she had worked so hard for the wealth; she wanted to leave a big legacy, not spend her money on the expenses of catastrophic illness.

With an IULI contract and some other types of policies as well, she can get what's called a chronic illness accelerated benefit rider, which again is a lot of terminology, a lot of words.

It means that the death benefit of the policy can be accelerated during a person's lifetime to pay for home healthcare, assisted living, and nursing home care. And what do we know about death benefit proceeds of life insurance? These are income tax-free. So if we're accelerating the death benefit payment, these are generally considered income tax-free as well. What's wrong with an income tax-free way to pay for long-term care?

By RONALD GELOK, with Adriane Berg

What we're able to do, and I don't want to say it's unique, but it does take some specialized knowledge to do this correctly, is to reverse engineer an investment grade IULI policy to perform in a superior fashion. We get better performance by designing the contract to provide the **least** amount of death benefit that we can get, so as to limit the mortality charges, limit the costs of insurance. We then have more money available for tax-free growth and tax-free distributions. If this appeals to you, look at the easy worksheets at www.fearfactorthebook.com.

Chapter 11

What Kind of a Team Do You Need to Navigate the Shark-Infested Waters That Lie Ahead?

We cover: An introduction to creating the ideal financial team; how the Gelok team can help, and which ancillary professionals might you need to add to your team.

You will discover:

> ➢ What fees awaits you?

> ➢ How long-term care problems can be solved—and NOT just financial issues

> ➢ How to avoid retirement pitfalls

> ➢ Beyond money: how a great retirement means life purpose, good health, and spiritual wealth

> ➢ Good stewardship for legacy building

What to do next:

Meet our team: Check out www.fearfactorthebook.com,
Create your Family Financial Tree and meet our family.

Ah, "shark-infested waters"... I know those are pretty strong words. I'm concerned that if you have had a bad experience in the past with your planning or investing, you will sit it out and just lose control over your financial future. That's why I want to make a preemptive strike and clue you in to dangers to help you navigate and feel strong the next time. I want there to be a next time.

In 2007 the average baby boomer had saved $77,000 for retirement. In 2014 it's $127,000. That's much better. There is serious money sitting in your accounts. Take control.

What awaits us when we finally go out there and we do our planning for retirement?

First, we have to face a fruit basket of professionals. It's hard to know exactly which one to use. Doctors refer you to specialists; many financial pros seek to do it all. If fact, most planners purport to cover five major areas for retirement—investing, taxes, legacy, long-term care, and income planning. I would like to meet a person who knows all there is to know about all five!

And if you did make all the correct choices, getting all your advisors to coordinate is a full-time job. One reason many people don't plan for retirement is the time and effort it takes to build a coordinated team. They have to see an accountant. They have to see a lawyer. They have to make those people talk to each other. They have to go to a financial planner, an insurance broker. We all agree we need a team, but it's very, very difficult to build our own team. So we fall for one stop shopping and feel relieved.

What to Look for in a Planner

There are many types of financial professionals you may work with. But to choose the correct team, regardless of background, education, licenses, and designations, there are a few fundamental attributes they must have.

To search for these attributes in others, I will tell you what we at Ronald Gelok & Associates try so hard to do right. That will not only allow me to show my pride in our TEAM, but give you a list of what to look for in other professionals.

I know that not all of you will become a client of Ronald Gelok & Associates, but I will rest easier knowing I helped you select the best available to you.

Building the Coordinated TEAM

Ask who is working on your case. Are they in-house or outside, and what are their roles and credentials?

It took years of identifying the right people with the right skill sets to form our TEAM. More than anything else, I looked for people with the attitude of caring about their clients. I hate to say through trial and error, but a bit through trial and error, we put together a team of professionals that work with our clients. Now, some of these are on salary, on our staff, and others of these are outside professionals.

By RONALD GELOK, with Adriane Berg

Make sure the TEAM will work with professionals you have used and like.

If a client says to me, "I've got an accountant I'm thrilled with" or "I've got an estate planning attorney who has been with our family for years," we can work with those professionals. But, if somebody says, "Ron, I've got an out-of-date will. It was done 30 years ago. There are trusts for minor children in it that are now adults, and I know I don't have a tax-planned will" or "I think maybe I need a revocable living trust," then we're going to make the introduction to an attorney who specializes in estate planning, and we're going to help quarterback that plan.

If you instinctively mistrust any member of the TEAM, move on.

The slogan of Ronald Gelok & Associates is Trust and Know-How. Let's unpack that. What is the importance of trust? It seems obvious, but I think it goes a little deeper than we think about when we're dealing with our retirement planning.

Last week we did one of our client appreciation events where we had 100+ clients come out and get together, and we gave them a dinner. We presented one of our client Ambassadors with an award, and I don't think I've ever met such a group of happy people in one room.

This trust was earned over time. But the way we're establishing trust with people is through complete transparency. You can feel when someone is cagey, even if you can't prove it.

Always insist on knowing all the fees; many are hidden or called by strange names.

We disclose the way we get paid. There are some things that we do that are fee-based. In that case, we're going to explain to a client the complete fee structure. Some things are commission-based, so if we make a recommendation that's in the best interest of the client, and that happens to be coming from a company that pays us a commission, we're going to disclose that, too.

In fact, one legitimate criticism of insurance products is that they are so complex you don't know how much and for what you are paying. Yes, I told you not to worry about insurance expenses, as long as you are making money. But I never said you should be in the dark. Get the facts.

By RONALD GELOK, with Adriane Berg

Learn how your advisors get clients

What's so startling and gratifying to me is we built our business through word of mouth. We don't advertise. You won't see me on television commercials or on billboards or in glossy magazine ads. We've built it all by one happy client telling a friend or a family member, "Go talk with Ron and his team." We call our clients our Ambassadors.

That's where the other part of our slogan, **Know-How,** works with trust. As we unpack that slogan, Trust and Know-How, we realize that a good TEAM is recognized because it does something right to earn trust.

For our TEAM, that "something right" is an EDUCATION mission. Just visit www.RonaldGelok.com and you will see how many live seminars and webinars we do, open to all.

How much education will your planner give you?

This goes back to my philosophy to never invest in what you don't understand. Look, I know I am suggesting insurance contracts, written so densely and confusingly that they are hard to grasp. But you can understand them with a TEAM willing to educate you.

Because of my training and background, I am able to pay attention to some of the minutia of the terms of insurance contracts. I'll have different wholesalers approach me telling me that I should be offering this product or that product to clients. You know what? The vast majority of these I throw in the garbage because they're one-sided or they're written in favor of an insurance company instead of the client.

Once I understand the details, I assure you I can explain them to you, and not only if you are a client. Come to our seminars, listen to our webinars, subscribe to my newsletter, follow my social media, and read my other books. Don't be a stranger.

That gets back to the mission to educate. When I was a college undergraduate, I went to Montclair State University, a great teacher's college. I thought I wanted to be a teacher at the time.

This is why I view my role as to educate and teach. I want you to be informed. If you're informed on pluses, minuses, costs, and benefits, then you know you're making the right decisions about what you're doing. I hate to say it, but I think there are too many people in our business who—how can I put it—lie by omission, meaning they may explain something, but they don't explain it in enough detail or they don't take time to make sure that the client gets it.

All the advisors on our team were trained by me to make sure that any client that they're counseling gets it, that they understand what's being explained to them backward and forward.

Does your advisor know taxes?

I graduated from the University of California's Hastings College of Law, which has one of the top tax law programs in the country, and so I'm always looking at the tax ramifications or tax implications of planning and investment decisions.

I think, in the world we live in today where taxes are so high, to fail to consider taxes is to operate at your own peril. Don't feel that because you have an accountant who does your taxes once a year it's enough. Our clients feel that in today's world just having a tax preparer is not good enough. And we have clients that are accountants themselves who agree.

Your TEAM may not be all financial professionals.

We've talked about the fact that we work with trusted outside sources like attorneys, accountants, and others. We work with our clients' own trusted financial professionals. But when it comes to building a team, there's a softer side of retirement, and that's the emotional issues such as where to move, how to keep up morale, how to help your aging parents, even how to travel.

A TEAM has to see a client as a whole person. We really get to know our clients, not just from the perspective of their finances, but knowing them as individuals, understanding what's important to them, and exploring what problems they want to solve. For example, 50% of all 60-year-olds have a living parent. They may be caring for their father or mother or both.

With the wrong TEAM, nobody will even bother to ask you, "Is your mom or dad still alive?" That's a critical question for many retirees. It's kind of hard to uproot and say, "I'm going to move to North Carolina or I'm going to move to Florida," if one's 92-year-old mother is in

By RONALD GELOK, with Adriane Berg

failing health in New Jersey. We look at all the issues that are of concern to you. And we are in contact with home health agencies, geriatric care managers, geriatricians, elder law attorneys, and senior moving specialists to add to the TEAM.

Clients have said to me, "You're the first person that ever asked me about my grandchild, and you're the first person that ever discovered that I have a grandchild who suffers from autism." Well, we need to know that because, if that's part of the planning to make special provisions for that grandchild, we want to be able to advise how to go about doing that.

A Note From Adriane

The Elder Law Attorney

One member of the team that you might not have considered is the elder law attorney. I was one of twenty-six lawyers who joined together decades ago to create a committee of the American Bar Association on Elder Law. Before then, there was really no such specialty. Trusts and estates attorneys might have helped. But most people with trusts and estates attorneys were quite well off. The average family had no such lawyer.

What you need is a coordinated TEAM that is dedicated to you.

Do you know the old saying, "There is no 'I' in TEAM"? Well, that's okay for Little League. For retirement planning, there is an I. You are the I. It should all be about your needs. Not commissions or fees. That will come. I know. I always put my clients first, and I make money.

You are a whole person with overlapping and sometimes seemingly conflicting goals. Over and over again I am asked, "Ronald, I want to give my grandchildren a leg up in life and, at the same time, I don't want to shortchange my own retirement.

"How can I generate the income I'll need over the next 35 years and at the same time be free to put together a plan to help fund my grandchild's education or to create an inherited Roth IRA for them one day?"

By RONALD GELOK, with Adriane Berg

Unfortunately, so much of what passes for retirement planning is done in a very disjointed, disconnected way. Do you work with a broker who looks at your investments, an attorney who did a will, and a tax professional that does your taxes every year? Do these professionals ever talk to one another? Is there a coordinated plan put together, an integrated system? I bet not. We try to fix that problem by taking a holistic approach and working with a team of professionals, whether they are professionals that a client already has on their team or whether we need to introduce them to the right people.

Taxes, another retirement shark

You know by now that one of the ways that we at Ronald Gelok & Associates distinguish ourselves is careful attention to the tax aspect of retirement planning, which is very often forgotten. If we're not careful, we leave ourselves vulnerable to taxes that we could describe as predatory or confiscatory.

I use the word *predatory* because, if you think about it, a shark is a predator. Just as if we were at the beach and a shark was spotted in the water, we get out of the water. If we know that there are provisions in the tax code that are traps for the unwary, we want to be able to deal with that ahead of time through proper planning.

Postretirement taxation is one area where people are lulled into a false sense of security much the same way somebody could be lying on a raft in shark-infested waters and think they're fine. Meanwhile, the sharks are underneath the raft.

Tax shark review:

1. I'm amazed how many people don't realize that in many states— New Jersey and New York, for example—there are state estate taxes. If we think we don't have to worry because we get a $5 million-plus federal estate tax threshold, and ignore, for example, that the state of New Jersey has got a $675,000 state estate tax threshold, we're leaving ourselves vulnerable.

2. Then there are the shark-infested tax waters when we withdraw from our 401(k)s and what happens when we have to make a Required Minimum Distribution. In our office we refer to 401(k)s, 403(b)s, 457 plans, and IRAs as being "tax-infested accounts" or "tax

hostile assets." When we first use these terms with people, they're a little taken aback. They'll say, "Well, I thought my 401(k) was the greatest thing because it allows me to grow my money tax-deferred."

I made the point that too much tax deferral is like a pact with the devil. Why? Because when the money comes out, it's coming out at some unknown future potentially higher tax rate. And if you draw out too fast, you can trigger massive taxation.

3. This is where we get into the whole overlooked area of distribution planning. When should we be drawing money out of the retirement accounts? Should we just follow conventional, tired wisdom that says wait until 70 1/2, or should we look at coordinating that decision with the age we intend to collect Social Security?

For example, we don't see anything wrong with taking some income distributions out of an IRA or 401(k) between 66 and 70, and delaying Social Security from 66 to 70 because by doing so, we make lifetime Social Security income 32% higher. Why? Social Security grows 8% for every year you delay taking it until age 70. Does your qualified plan earn a guaranteed 8% a year?

Make our relationship ongoing.

Maybe it's overkill, but we are with our clients a good deal. We have seminars almost every week. We have client appreciation events. We use Skype if they go on vacation and need us.

We post on Facebook, Twitter, and LinkedIn five days a week with an article or a hint or tip, or just a book review. We post webinars you can access 24/7, and news you can use, usually articles in all areas of life health, travel, anything that really is relevant to what retirement means in your life. I think that's why the people at the client appreciation meeting are pretty happy people.

We have clients referring across generations. I can think of one family where the great-grandparent was a client. The daughter was a client. The grandson was a client, and we did some 529 plans for education funding for a great-grandchildren. It's nice when we're able to work with a family across generations and do family meetings.

Meet our team: Check out www.fearfactorthebook.com. Create your Family Financial Tree and meet our family.

By RONALD GELOK, with Adriane Berg

Chapter 12

How Does Overcoming F.E.A.R. and Making Smart Decisions in Your Money Life Spill Over to All of Your Retirement Decisions?

We cover: You will be amazed at how rapidly formerly unsolvable issues, such as where and when you want to retire and what you will do after retirement, will be solved once you have a perpetual financial system that never runs out of money no matter how long you live.

You will discover:

> ➢ A review of F.E.A.R. as it relates to money

> ➢ How F.E.A.R. also relates to other issues

> ➢ How dancing to your own drummer and believing in yourself is essential to a free and amazing retirement

> ➢ How vanquishing the F.E.A.R. Factors inspires others

What to do next:

> ➢ Listen to the outstanding guests and visit the website www.SuperAgingToday.com and get inspired.

Way back at the beginning of this book, we lamented that people do not spend time planning for retirement, partially because they can't answer the tough questions like where they want to live after retirement or even what they plan to do after retirement. How does a system of tax-free income help answer those life questions?

I'll give you an example. Not so long ago, a husband and wife came into my office on the verge of getting into an argument over investment risk. The husband's point of view was that the market keeps going up, and he wants to keep participating in the upside of the market. He does not want to go "safe" with bonds. The wife's view of safety was FDIC-insured CDs. She said, "We can't afford to go through another 2008, and we need to have a strategy to not lose 30% to 40% of our retirement savings."

My role was not just to ask the boilerplate questions about where do you want to live, how do you want to spend your time, is travel

By RONALD GELOK, with Adriane Berg

important to you, and how much time do you want to spend with the grandkids. Those are important questions, but first we had to put together a financial plan to make them both happy. My role was to get them both on the same page, so they had clarity of mind to answer the questions. You see, the money plan comes before the answers, in some families.

What did we do? We identified what the real problem was, a retirement income gap. We knew how much was going to be coming in the way of Social Security income for the two of them. They had both worked at many jobs over the years. The husband had worked for six different employers, yet none of them offered a traditional defined benefit pension plan. There was a gap between what was coming from Social Security and what was needed to pay the bills.

We looked toward insurance contracts that offered guarantees to generate income. Once we knew that the income gap was solved, that we had a system in place to cover the shortfall between real-world expenses and Social Security, the wife was okay taking risks with some of the money.

We have a saying in our office: "Security brings surety." If you're secure financially, you get surer about the rest of what you want to do with your life. People might say, gee, I'm going to move to Florida, California, or Europe. Can they? How can you select a home, even know what price range you're in, if you don't know your financial future? Once that's set, then the other questions can be answered.

According to the AARP, the number one goal after retirement for most people is to travel. What does it mean? It doesn't mean anything until you know how much you can spend on trips or whether you can rent an apartment abroad, or other items that would provide your ideal retirement. Then you can really make a plan.

But most people are derailed by F.E.A.R. Factors. They don't want to know the truth about their finances because they are afraid that will kill their dreams.

To me it's just the opposite. It's part of my belief system that if people can free themselves and think on their own financially, it's going to help them pursue their retirement dreams.

By RONALD GELOK, with Adriane Berg

They're not going to be tied down. They're not just going to give lip service to the desire to write a book or travel around the world or start a nonprofit organization. They're really going to do it.

I honor my clients, year after year, who have broken the mold. The ability to think on your own with respect to your money carries over to other parts of your retirement life.

Most people believe that if they had enough net worth, they would be free to live as they please. We all want to be free to do the things that we love to do, to pursue our interests, to be able to spend time with our family, with our children, our grandchildren, our spouse, to spend part of the year in a warmer climate, or to fund our grandkids' education or help them buy their first car.

Our point of view is that if you stop running with the herd, if you start thinking for yourself, if you seek out advisors like the advisors on our team, you're going to position yourself to both be free financially and of limiting beliefs, conventional thinking, live the life of which you've always dreamed.

We've seen it over and over again. An individual or a couple plans a great and creative retirement, and it rubs off on all the family.

Other people see them and ask, "How did you manage to go around the world, or start a business, or a foundation, or buy a second home? They answer, "By trusting our advisors and by thinking outside the box."

So what if you find out that you don't have enough to afford your dreams? First, you maximize what you do have and get a foundation. Then, you get creative. We can help with ways to fund the book you want to write or the trip you want to take by thinking outside the box. Become a travel writer, build a house yourself, enlist friends in a new business, and fund a foundation with online fundraising. Don't just read about those remarkable people that accomplish wonderful things after age 60. Be one of those people. Be F.E.A.R.less.

By RONALD GELOK, with Adriane Berg

Chapter 13

How Does Discovering Your Financial Blind Spots Lead to Making Better Financial Decisions?

What we cover: We are all unable to see certain dangers in our plan. When they are noted, we can take care of them, and we can prosper. What we don't see are our blind spots, and they can destroy our retirement. Let's identify the most frequent blind spots.

What you will discover: The big blind spots:
  ➢ taxes
  ➢ risk
  ➢ income gap
  ➢ catastrophic illness

What to do next:

  ➢ Visit www.RonaldGelok.com./FEARFactor. You'll discover your blind spots. I assure you it's going to be a real eye-opener.

Let's say you're driving down the highway or freeway and you start to change lanes. And so you glance at your rearview mirror. You glance in your side-view mirror. Your turn signal is on. You start easing over, and all of a sudden somebody is leaning on the horn at you, and you scoot back to your lane as quick as you can. But meanwhile, your chest is pounding and you've got an adrenaline rush, right?
You say, "Oh my gosh. I didn't even see that guy. He was in my blind spot."

Not seeing somebody in a blind spot can result in a devastating automobile accident, and the same is true with one's finances. If there are blind spots that we're ignoring or cannot see at all, there could be irreversible financial consequences. We view our role as not only to advise clients on the problems of which they are aware, but to point out the blind spots that they may be overlooking or not considering.

By RONALD GELOK, with Adriane Berg

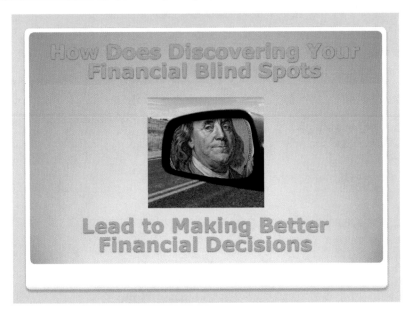

Tax blind spots: Oh, not again!

Yes, again. If you have grasped the importance of tax savings, skip this section. But if you did not do the worksheets on taxes, read this section; you need the drill.

A lot of us are lulled into a false sense of security when it comes to estate taxes because we know that a few years ago we came dangerously close to having the federal estate tax threshold dropped to $1 million with anything over $1 million taxed at a 55% rate. That was scheduled to go into effect January 1, 2013.

Well, that didn't happen. At the last minute, the end result of the fiscal cliff negotiations included a $5 million federal estate tax threshold indexed for inflation. Now is that going to be permanent? Well, who knows? The politicians have changed the federal estate tax threshold 12 times in the last 15 years.

But the blind spot that a lot of people are ignoring or forgetting about is that many, many states—New York and New Jersey included—have state estate taxes. Anything over $675,000 in New Jersey is subject to the state estate taxes when it passes to the next generation. This is one example of a blind spot.

For married couples, for example, it can be fairly easily corrected just by doing a tax-planned will, which includes a marital trust for the benefit of the surviving spouse. That trust, in effect, gets its own estate tax exemption. But sometimes we don't know what we don't know, and that's one example of just one blind spot.

A tax blind spot that I mentioned several times is how much tax we pay when we withdraw from our 401(k)s or other qualified plans. Let's take a look at that blind spot once again.

At age 70 1/2 the Required Minimum Distribution that a person would have to take out as a percentage of qualified assets is 3.65%, so that means for each $100,000 of IRA, 401(k), or retirement plan money, you'll have to pull out $3,650. But, by age 80, that's up over 5%. Each year, as you get older, you're required to take a little bit more out.

Blind Spots: Required Minimum Distribution

Table 4: Required Minimum Distributions

Age	Factor	Required Minimum Distribution
70	27.4	3.65%
71	26.5	3.77%
72	25.6	3.91%
73	24.7	4.05%
74	23.8	4.20%
75	22.9	4.37%
76	22.0	4.55%
77	21.2	4.72%
78	20.3	4.93%
79	19.5	5.13%

We're often misguidedly advised that if you're in your 60s, you shouldn't take any money out of your qualified plans or retirement accounts because that's going to incur an income tax liability. But what's wrong with taking some money out of those plans when you're in your 60s if that money is going to be taxed at a lower rate than if you wait until you're 70? What we don't realize is that too much tax deferral, the subject of a prior chapter, can be like a pact with the devil.

By RONALD GELOK, with Adriane Berg

We have risk blind spots, too.

You can have the best estate plan in the world, the best legal documents in the world. We could put together the best distribution plan to figure out how and when you should be taking money out of the tax qualified retirement plans. But if we ignore the issue of investment risk, what do we really accomplish? We must address those risk factors up front and seek to minimize or reduce those risk factors.

Those of you who paid attention in prior chapters understand the issues of guarantees and floors and that they are not too good to be true.

With investments that directly involve securities, there are no guarantees against loss or of performance—past performance is no guarantee of future results. If a client says, "Look, I'm really craving some type of guarantee that will protect a portion of my retirement savings against loss and would give me some level of guaranteed income," we look to offerings from insurance companies that do just that.

We can use a fixed annuity tied to a market index. In that case, your account doesn't go backward when the market goes backwards. At the same time, you are capturing interest credits linked to the S&P 500 in the good years, keeping those gains, avoiding losses in the down years, with a lifetime income guarantee rider that will compound at 6% or 6.5% or 7% per year to meet future income needs.

Income gap blind spots

For many, a blind spot is the income gap. A generation ago, it seemed like retirement planning was a lot easier because 82% of people then had paychecks for life in the form of traditional defined benefit pensions—mailbox money every month. Now it's the exact opposite. Over 80% of us don't have pensions.

Advances in medical technology are keeping people alive longer and longer. At the same time, people don't have guaranteed income for life unless they put together a system to create that.

We need to put a system in place that gives guarantees to cover the income gap. It's pretty hard to live on Social Security alone. If we look

By RONALD GELOK, with Adriane Berg

at what your expenses are and what your expenses are likely to be in the future, and we have a solution to cover the gap between those expenses and what's coming from Social Security, we're solving a big, big problem.

One of the hardest questions to answer of any financial planner is how much money do I need, so you can see whether you have a gap in the first place. That's why you need somebody that you trust, who has the know-how to work backward and forward with you. How much do you need? Here's what you realistically can accomplish with this much risk. Do you need more? Are you willing to take on more risk, or are you satisfied? These are the real questions of real clients that have real fears.

Catastrophic illness blind spot

Even with a great system, if we ignore the blind spot of your health failing, we accomplish nothing. Remember the story of my own parents.

If we hadn't planned, once that Alzheimer's diagnosis was made, their entire legacy could have been lost to the expenses of the nursing home. That's where my mother ultimately passed away, in an Alzheimer's unit of a nursing home. Now, granted, I found her the best nursing home I could find, but she got to a point physically where there was no other choice but care in that type of setting.

Today, most people do survive a stroke, and they need care for years and years. And so it's not just dementia and Alzheimer's and Parkinson's, but it can be heart attacks and strokes because medicine is so good. Seven out of ten seniors will need some type of long-term care. Then we must explore solutions that involve thinking outside the box.

Long-term care insurance

For example, somebody may say to me, "Look; I've already looked into traditional long-term care insurance, and I don't like it."

I'll ask, "Well, why don't you like it?"

They'll say, "You know, the premiums are not guaranteed. My friend had a 52% increase in costs on his long-term care 2 years ago, and I

By RONALD GELOK, with Adriane Berg

just don't like the idea of having a policy in effect for 5, 10, 15, 20 years and then getting hit with a 50% or 60% premium increase."

I would agree. That doesn't make sense as a strategy in my mind either, but there are other things to look at.

There's single premium, sometimes referred to as single deposit combination long-term care life plans. For example:

ALL VALUES AND BENEFITS ARE GUARANTEED[1]

One-Time Premium	$100,000.00	Return of Premium Benefit	$100,000.00
Total Long-Term Care Benefits	$246,159.00	**Covered Expenses**	
Monthly Maximum Benefit[2]	$3,418.88	0-Day Elimination Period	90-Day Elimination Period
Benefit Duration	6 Years	• Home health care • Care coordination	• Nursing home facility • Assisted living facility
Inflation Benefit Option	Rejected	• Caregiver training[3] • Home modification[3]	• Facility hospice care • International benefit
Initial Death Proceeds (Before Minimum Death Benefit)	$100,000.00[4]	• Durable medical equipment[3] • Adult day care center	

Life insurance policies that have a chronic illness accelerated benefit rider can be used to accelerate the death benefit to pay for long-term care.

We even have, for people who are completely uninsurable, access to programs where we can put a guarantee or a rider on a retirement account that can double income in the event of the need for home health care, assisted living, or long-term care.

Too often, we don't know what we don't know in terms of effective strategies to protect ourselves and our family from the devastating costs of catastrophic illness. Our view is that our clients deserve to know about them, and they need to put a system in place to deal with it.

A Note From Adriane

The #1 Blind Spot

There is no doubt in my mind that today's greatest blind spot is our longevity. When I was a teenager, the line was "Never trust anybody over 30." Thirty was too old to be cool.

By RONALD GELOK, with Adriane Berg

You might remember the Pulitzer Prize-winning play *Marty* by Paddy Chayefsky. In the play, sisters are talking about being "over the hill" and "out to pasture." The dialogue revealed they were 55 years old. In *Sunset Boulevard*, Gloria Swanson played a great actress deranged because she was marginalized by age. In the movie she was removed from her home to an institution. She too was in her 50s. I just saw a *People* magazine feature of Helen Mirren age 69, in a bikini. Times have changed.

Most of us were not brought up in the culture of longevity. Sixty-five was the retirement age. It was the age of Social Security, the senior citizen, the early-bird special, the crotchety old man, the old crone woman.

Current television has not done much to improve the image. So we have to do that on our own. If you don't believe in your own longevity and the fabulous prospects of the years ahead, why bother to plan to live those years to the hilt?

If you don't acknowledge the fun, fulfilling lifestyle, contribution, and thrills (yes, thrills) you can have in your 70s, you probably won't have them. Today, the average lifespan is around age 84 to 87 in the United States. This is somewhat effected by gender, location, life experience, career, and of course genetics. Most people today die of a heart attack. And they otherwise **die healthy**. It means you can live life up to the last moment. Why not plan for yourself instead of leaving the possibilities up to fate alone. Fate will take over if it wants to. Don't tempt it. Wake up to your longevity, and make the most of it.

Visit www.fearfactorthebook.com. You'll discover your blind spots. I assure you it's going to be a real eye-opener.

By RONALD GELOK, with Adriane Berg

Chapter 14

Epilogue: Take the F.E.A.R. Factor Quiz

So, have you beaten the F.E.A.R. Factor? Take this True and False Quiz, and then visit www.fearfactorthebook.com to find out.

True or False

a. An annuity is a security like a stock or bond.

b. Medicare pays for skilled nursing at home if you have a stroke or long-term care need like Parkinson's or Alzheimer's.

c. The cost of investing $100,000 in an indexed annuity is about double of buying an indexed mutual fund.

d. When you borrow too much against an insurance policy cash value, it could lapse and you automatically lose the death benefit.

By RONALD GELOK, with Adriane Berg

e. The death benefit your heirs get from an insurance policy is always inherited tax-free.

f. There are no more estate taxes.

g. When you borrow from your insurance policy, it's tax-free.

h. If you borrow from an insurance policy and don't pay it back before you pass away, the policy will lapse.

i. Annuities require you to give up a lump sum of money on return for monthly income.

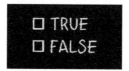

By RONALD GELOK, with Adriane Berg

j. An indexed universal life insurance policy means that some money goes to a death benefit against which you can borrow and some to an account that earns interest linked to the growth of a stock index like the S&P.

k. Long-term care insurance puts you in danger of paying escalating premiums all your life until you make a claim against the policy.

l. Riders are gimmicks that insurance companies tack on to annuities or if their investments go poorly.

Epilogue: Register for the F.E.A.R. Factor Webinar Series

The F.E.A.R. Factor:

15 Minutes to Your Ideal Retirement

Don't Base Your Future On False Evidence About Retirement

Register for this 12 Webinar Series with strategies to build your ideal retirement.

There is no cost and no obligation.

Here is what you will discover to create your ideal retirement:

- The 7 questions which reveal fatal financial mistakes that could ruin your retirement
- How to overcome herd mentality which keeps you buying high and selling low, or remaining entirely stagnant
- How to create a tax-free income stream before and after retirement
- How to protect yourself and your loved ones from healthcare costs, medical bankruptcies and impoverishment
- How to borrow from specialized insurance policies tax-free and still earn income on borrowed funds
- How to participate in the equity markets with guarantees against loss
- How to build a financial team even if you're not Rockefeller
- How the Roth IRA works for and against you, so you can make the right choice
- Why 401(k)s and IRAs tax deferral may be a pact with the devil

Frequently asked questions on these webinars:

Q. Am I buying something when I register for your webinar? Will salesman hounds me to death after I register?

A. You are buying nothing, spending nothing and signing up for nothing except the webinars themselves. At the end of each webinar you will hear verbal a invitation to receive a complimentary consultation from Ronald Gelok and Associates. You will not be called unless you request a call. You will be invited to special events like

By RONALD GELOK, with Adriane Berg

luncheons, library educational series, additional webinars and book signings.

Q. Exactly what is the primary business of Ronald Gelok and Associates and why are you doing the webinars?

A. Ronald Gelok and Associates our financial advisors that help you strategize your retirement future starting at any age. Many of our clients are actually post-retirees who want to make the most of their nest eggs. Ronald Gelok is also an attorney with the tax background. We have been in practice for over 20 years and are licensed to provide money management, annuities, insurance and many other financially appropriate financial products and services.

Q. Why is Ronald Gelok and Associates offering these webinars?

A. We are extremely education oriented and do most of our outreach to the public through seminars and webinars. This series of 12 Webinars is a valuable addition to this book.